YOU'VE GOT TO
BELIEVE
YOU'RE GOING
TO BE
OK

From Fear to Faith

A Testimony by

LORRAINE BROWN

*Faith*Source
PUBLISHING

YOU'VE GOT TO BELIEVE YOU'RE GOING TO BE OK:
FROM FEAR TO FAITH

Published by Faith Source Publishing, Inc.
info@faithsourcepublishing.com
(312) 741-3777

Note on Quoted Email Messages: The author received permission to include the email messages from family and friends that appear throughout this book. In most cases last names have been omitted in respect to the sender(s), although some senders offered permission to use their whole names. In addition, the author has centered all Bible block quotations within emails and also added Bible source citations in emails that quoted from the Bible but did not include a source citation, including these citations in brackets.

Interior Layout: Mandi Cofer, thetinytypesetter.com
Cover Design: Kristen Ingebretson, kristening.com
Front cover images © Shutterstock

Paperback ISBN#: 978-1-7338988-0-5

Library of Congress Control Number: 2019903711

Dedication

To my loving husband, Greg, who stood by me in strength and faith every step of the way, loving me enormously; to every single person who prayed for me during this challenging journey; to my faithful family and friends, as well as my lifelong family doctor, William Kehoe, all of whom spoke constant words of encouragement, wisdom, and truth into my spirit as I navigated the road before me!

Author's Note

This is a real-life story about hope and expectation; about the longing in our hearts to be healed and whole; about what to do while waiting for our prayers to be answered. We are all in our own personal "waiting room." What is it that you are waiting for today? No matter what it might be, it is my prayer that this book will help you to believe that you are going to be OK!

Contents

Introduction

The waiting room is never a comfortable place to be. Regardless of which side of the room you are on, you can experience many uncomfortable moments there. However, the waiting room is not forever—and you are not alone! God isn't sitting by passively, watching. God is a good God who cares about every detail of your life. God is waiting too! He is waiting for you to call—and He will answer!

As we wait, we are thrust into the unknown. Our minds can wander, and our thoughts can run away. Our attention span can become fragmented by the activity of the surroundings. We do quite a bit of waiting if life, don't we? We wait for the airplane: Will our loved one arrive safely? We wait for the phone to ring: Will we get the job? Will the news be good or bad? Will the wayward child return? Will the outcome of the surgery be successful? Will the treatment work? Will healing come? Our patience is tried. Our faith is put to the test.

My story is about the fight for my life. It is a story of challenges and triumphs—faith versus fear . . . a story of choices! It is really God's story—the Author of Life. And this, then, is a letter from Him to you, transcribed by me. I'm just a character in this story. Each chapter has been touched, changed, brightened, and blessed by the God who wrote this long before I transcribed it. Each thought is punctuated by the mighty power of God.

This letter is a tool—with the purpose of helping readers repair or rebuild something broken by fortifying the minds of those who dare to retain what is spoken here.

I also want to share here that you yourself are a letter! I love what the apostle Paul wrote in the New Testament: "But you are our letter, and you are in our hearts for everyone to read and understand" (2 Corinthians 3:2 CEV).

God is looking for people who are steadfastly seeking Him, whose hearts He can work in, and whose lives He can fix and heal! So as we think about our own stories as being a tool, let us remember that this tool is for the purpose of sharing the power of God's great work in our lives and for His power to be manifest in the lives of others as well. As each life is fixed and healed, each story will also play a part in more lives becoming whole.

"Cancer?! Why?
Of all people, why you?"

After I began sharing with others that I had cancer, these are the words I heard from several friends in some form or another: "You have such healthy habits and take such good care of yourself. How could this happen to you?"

I have to admit: those same words ran through my mind as well. Why me? Yet the question "Why me?" seemed to be a waste of time. When you're stuck in the middle of something bad and faced with a fight in front of you, why get stuck in the "Why me?" mind-set? I didn't have time to sit and reason through the days, months, or years leading up to that moment. It was time to seize the moment and forge ahead with a plan of attack— and to conquer! It was time to humble myself before God . . . to call upon Him and trust that He would uphold me with His mighty hand, because I knew He promises to do so in His Word. I needed to trust—really trust that there is a path to victory. I faced a great storm and I didn't know the outcome. I had to trust Him for that. I had to ride on His wings as He carried me through.

I pray that you will not get stuck in the circumstance you are in right now by dwelling on the problem but rather that you will think beyond this situation. In Jeremiah 29:11, God's Word says that He knows the plans He has for you—not for harm or calamity, but to prosper you, plans for a hope and a future. Do you believe it? If you do, I urge you to receive what He said and to focus on Him—trusting in Him and leaning on Him with all your heart . . . not your own human ways of reasoning. Our ways are so limited.

Take a moment to think about these incredible verses:

> And we know that in all things God works for the good of those who love him, who have been called according to his purpose. (Romans 8:28 NIV)

> "For I know the plans I have for you," declares the LORD, "plans to prosper you and not to harm you, plans to give you hope and a future. Then you will call on me and come and pray to me, and I will listen to you. You will seek me and find me when you seek me with all your heart." (Jeremiah 29:11-13 NIV)

As declared by these verses, I knew there were steps required of me during this dramatic episode of my life. I also needed to remember not to focus only on this "scene" . . . this moment.

Today is only one page and your current situation is only one chapter within *your* story. You are in the middle of it right now—the middle of the story of your life. What you do in this moment and how you handle it will play a role in the outcome. Your beliefs, your attitudes, and your decisions all become a factor. In the writing of your story, how will the next scene play out if you are doubtful, negative, and hopeless, and if you lose faith? How will it play out if you stand firmly and faithfully on God's promises—without doubt, and believing and receiving His power to deliver you and trusting Him for your future? Which scene would you prefer to have become the reality in your story? As silly as that last question might seem, it is a valid one because there is something required to receive that reality: unwavering faith in God, who says, ". . . I am the Lord, who heals you" (Exodus 15:26 NIV).

In the twists and turns of any story, some moments will cause wide-eyed suspense. I can attest to that! Yet the suspense can be turned into wide-eyed AWE of God as you stay firmly planted in Him and He leads you to the next chapter. As you look to God and stay positive in faith, you can continue in hopeful expectation.

Turn the page to begin reading God's letter to you . . .

CHAPTER 1

The Call

It was a Friday afternoon in September—9/11/15. The voice on the other side of the phone was the oncologist's nurse practitioner: "I'm sorry . . . the doctor is out of the country, but he wanted me to call you immediately. The news is not good. The cancer has come back to two different areas and you need to have chemo right away."

My knees buckled and the weight of my body forced me to the floor. I felt as if someone just clenched my stomach and squeezed the air out of me. I paused . . . a long time. The nurse began to speak words of encouragement, but all I could hear in my head was the news she'd given me! I replied out of disbelief, "How could this be?!"

Six months earlier I had undergone a total hysterectomy for a uterine tumor. It was the very aggressive type. However, it was in the earliest stage and very small. The surgery revealed it had not spread, and all the pathology reports came back showing that I was completely free of cancer. Even so, I was advised to have four short radiation treatments that would protect me and bring the chance of any recurrence down to less than 1 percent.

After recovering from the surgery, I was doing great and all my follow up exams were excellent. But I eventually started experiencing some cramping, which led to my doctor ordering a CT scan. The phone call from the nurse practitioner was the bearer of the unwanted result of that scan. She said that it was indeed back and that sometimes this occurs—and there is no clear explanation. She went on to say that many patients had been with them for quite a long time and were doing alright.

I replied, "Alright is not good enough." Then I started to cry, saying, "I just can't believe this is happening."

As she realized that her kind attempt to comfort me wasn't working, she offered me a prescription for Ativan (an anti-anxiety med). I rejected that immediately within and snapped back, "I don't have anxiety! I'm in shock and disbelief, and I need time to process the information! I have my faith and it is better than any anti-anxiety drug!"

Even though my tone really didn't exhibit an anxiety-free attitude, the nurse remained calm and compassionate. She told me to take the weekend to process everything, and she said she'd check back with me on Monday.

I don't know about you, but it seems like bad news almost always comes late in the day on a Friday!

The weekend felt surreal. I'd experience moments of intense fear. Then strength and courage would rise up and replace the fear—only to have it slap me back down into a fetal position, as if in a boxing match and unable to defend myself . . . weakened by the thoughts that kept crowding my brain.

I cried in my husband's arms as he held me tightly. I wanted to crawl inside of him and become a part of him, hiding away and sheltered, where nobody or nothing could touch me. Tears flowed a like river until they dried up. Then came conversations about what to do and questions to write down for my next visit with the doctor, accompanied by fearful thoughts of all the what-if's. I found myself on an emotional roller coaster—in a battle . . . a fight of faith versus fear! I knew I had to get it together, but I also knew I could not do it alone. This is where my faith needed to kick in. I needed a supernatural infusion of strength!

I was advised by friends and family, as well as my family doctor, to get a second and third opinion. And so the research began. I reached out to two more top hospitals in my area and was able to get in to see their specialists. Over a period of two weeks I ran from office to office, dropping off copies of test results and pathology reports, and meeting with the doctors for additional exams. One doctor in particular gave me such dire results that I'd rather not repeat what he said. He basically gave me no hope and then left the office. I sat there shaking as uncontrollable tears poured out of me. His associate had a look of disbelief on her face as she watched him leave and close the door behind him. Her jaw drooped, and her eyes reflected the question in her mind—the question that I quickly half cried, half shouted: "How can he be so heartless?" She rolled her stool close to me and put her hand on my shoulder and said, "Don't listen to that. We have plenty of patients who have had this disease and they have come through this and are doing well. You can't let what he said affect how you think or believe." I felt grateful to her as I thanked her and replied, "I do not accept what he said. He is NOT God! He has NO right to talk to me in that manner." I thanked her for her compassion, and I asked for the return of all of my test results because I would not be going back there.

That appointment was the only one I went to all alone. My husband was at work, and by that time I had been used to visiting oncologists and was sure that this would go just about the same as the others. This time, though, I walked back to my car in tears, talking to God: "Why did this have to happen, God? What am I to think of this?" Oh, how I wished my husband was there with me! When I got in the car, I dialed my family doctor and he was able to talk me through the pain and fear and the what-if's. After his wise and gentle words of encouragement, he said:

"Lorraine, you've got to believe you're going to be OK!"

It was exactly what I needed to hear. Without hesitation, as if a light switch had flipped on in my head, I said, "I do! I do believe I'm going to be OK!" From that moment on, every time fear gripped me, I replayed his words in my mind and I echoed my reply to him! I had to do this often because fear kept creeping around. I needed all the encouragement I could get, so we rallied all our trusted friends and family whom we knew we could count on to pray—really pray—and the faith journey began!

CHAPTER 2

Embarking into a Foreign Land

All of the doctors that I consulted with confirmed the original diagnosis: a very serious situation that needed immediate treatment! Now the decision was before me. Should I take the traditional approach? Opt for the natural approach? What would best suit me? After extensive research I chose the traditional route that the first oncologist had recommended—chemotherapy. This decision did not come easy. It was in fact a choice that went against everything I was—a person who had never so much as taken a pain reliever, but now about to embark into the foreign land of chemo!

Several days before my first scheduled treatment date, Anthony—my dear friend Jaime's husband—called to encourage me. He said, "Lorraine, do you know what faith is?"

I thought, *What kind of question is that?!*

He continued to share that we are all given "the measure of faith" by God (Romans 12:3 KJV). We can access that faith but "We need to believe," he said.

Anthony then shared Mark 11:23-24 (NIV): "God's Word says: 'Truly I tell you, if anyone says to this mountain, "Go, throw yourself into the sea," and does not doubt in their heart but believes that what they say will happen, it will be done for them.' This is in God's Word! If it is in God's Word, it is true!"

I had no problem with this. I believed God's Word then and I still do today!

Anthony went on very passionately, this time quoting Romans 10:17 (NKJV) and continuing with his comments: "'So then faith comes by hearing, and hearing by the word of God.' We need to speak what we want to receive. We need to believe God and reach out and take what He offers. Jesus has already completed His work on the cross. Do you believe He died for your sins by taking your place on the cross?"

I replied, "Yes!"

"How did you receive this forgiveness?"

"I believed it and I said it and I accepted it. I reached out and took it."

"Right, then do you believe He also died for your sicknesses and took upon Himself in His very own body all of your diseases?"

"Yes!" I almost shouted. "I do!"

"Then how will you access your healing, which has already been accomplished for you?"

Now I exclaimed, "I'll believe it and speak it and receive it! I'll reach out and take it!"

"Yes, because His Word says: 'But he was wounded for our transgressions, he was bruised for our iniquities: the chastisement of our peace was upon him; and with his stripes we are healed,'" Anthony said, quoting from Isaiah 53:5 (KJV).

"Take it, Lorraine. Take your healing! And never doubt!" In an excited voice he then quoted from James 1:6-7 (NIV): "The Word says that we are not to doubt 'because the one who doubts is like a wave of the sea, blown and tossed by the wind. That person should not expect to receive anything from the Lord.' So never doubt! Believe, Lorraine, believe!"

This brought back to mind what my doctor had said: *"You've got to believe you're going to be OK!"*

I admit, that phone conversation was not an easy one for me. Although grateful for Anthony's compassion and his concern for me, as well as his passion for God's Word and his desire to speak it loud and clear into my spirit, I hung up the phone wondering whether or not I should even have chemo. *Is this doubt? If God has healed me, then maybe I don't need chemo. If I proceed with chemo, am I double-minded? Now what? What choice do I make?* I called out to God for a clear answer and I waited for His reply. I spoke to my husband and to faithful friends and asked for prayer over my concerns. I even approached an alternative treatment hospital in case I would decide to go in a different direction. I kept feeling led back to my original choice of the hospital and oncologist who already knew me and was ready to lead me through this journey.

However, it wasn't until the last minute—*on a Friday afternoon,* four days before the scheduled start date—that I came to a decision. My husband got home from work that Friday, and we talked through all of the logistics. As we talked, we acknowledged first that we lived only four blocks from my original choice. Even so, I was still not 100 percent convinced. Then the phone rang. It was the social worker *at that hospital* asking if I needed any type of support. After I spoke briefly with her, the phone rang again. It was a trusted confidant who had previously been in charge of the women's center *at that hospital*. She said that if she were to select anyone, she would select the doctor I had seen there! As I was hanging up with her, another call clicked in, and on the other end was the woman who ran the wig center *at that hospital*, saying they just received a new shipment of high-quality wigs, and if I could get there today or tomorrow, I would have first dibs. I told her I would be there in twenty minutes. I got there in ten!

Another affirmation soon followed. While at the wig center, the nutritionist in the same office area saw me and invited me to sit with her to discuss my diet and supplements. Although it took some time for me to make my treatment decision, friends and family confessed that they believed all along that this hospital was the best choice for many reasons, not to mention the close proximity. Decision made! Deep breath! Date set! Perfect ending to a very "wigged out" day!

Next . . . time to get it together . . . gather my composure . . . take control of my emotions. The journey was about to begin—a weekly visit for eighteen weeks of intravenous injections! Would I have enough veins to hold up for eighteen weeks? What was to be expected? The unknown was knocking at my door—a door being forced open as I pushed back emotionally. Yet I realized that I had to open it and let the medicine in.

CHAPTER 3

Rallying the Troops

I began to rally the troops by sending out emails to my dear family and friends, requesting their prayers and emotional support for the battle set before me:

From: Lorraine
To: All
Date: October 20, 2015 1:40 PM
Subject: Health Update

Dear family and friends,

I'm sorry that I didn't get the update out sooner. I know you are praying! I am so blessed!!!

The last few weeks have flown by and I've been busy running to all kinds of appointments, gathering info, and picking up and dropping off records, etc. However, I'm grateful that I got to see three top doctors, including the one who is already my oncologist.

When I visited the others, they said that they have a great deal of respect for my oncologist. This should have given me great peace, but I still had to pursue other possible options. The Lord, knowing me intimately, made it clear to me yesterday that I'm in the right place with the right specialist and medical team. Being only four blocks away might have been a clear sign to some right from the beginning, but again . . . God knows me! ;)

Perhaps I was hoping that someone might say "No, this isn't cancer." In fact that is what I was hoping. That did not happen. They all concurred that this is that same "serous carcinoma" that was removed during surgery, recurring in other places in the body (on my omentum and transverse colon). This is not something that can be surgically removed. It has to be attacked with chemo.

It's a mystery based on the clean report and successful surgery I had back in February. It had not penetrated the wall of the uterus, no lymph node involvement, no cancer anywhere, and all clean blood work, etc. My chance for recurrence was supposed to be less than 1%. For this reason it has been difficult to grasp.

Bottom line . . . I need chemo. This is a very aggressive form of cancer. It is crucial to go after it intensely.

So . . . my treatment starts tomorrow and it will be once a week for 18 weeks! It goes in cycles of three. The first visit will be a long day with two drugs, then the next two weeks will be short days with only one drug. Then that same cycle repeats throughout treatment. Greg will be with me tomorrow. I'm blessed to have his tenderness and his warm, strong hand to hold!

It's quite a battle ahead but I'll keep reflecting on this:

"The Lord will fight for you; you need only to be still."
(Exodus 14:14 NIV)

I'm so grateful that so many of you are wanting to help us and have asked me to let you know what we need. At this point I think I'll need to get through the first treatment in order to know. I promise I will let you know and I will let people help. I am overwhelmed with gratitude that so much love is pouring over us through all of you! God's love and mercy is at work. You are beautiful!

I will keep you updated so that you know how to pray. Please pray now, for tomorrow to go well and for me to tolerate this treatment extremely well with no negative or adverse reactions. Please pray for the entire medical staff caring for me . . . that they will be precise and will do their job with amazing excellence . . . that God will be their wisdom and expertise! I pray for God's presence to be felt there, not only by me but by everyone. I pray for the other people there too. I pray that those who are afraid or unsure will be comforted.

I will stand on the promises of God's Word. I continue to trust for His healing in my body!

[What, what would have become of me] had I not believed that I would see the Lord's goodness in the land of the living! Wait and hope for and expect the Lord; be brave and of good courage and let your heart be stout and enduring. Yes, wait for and hope for and expect the Lord.
(Psalm 27:13-14 AMPC)

This is my verse for today:

> "You will not have to fight this battle. Take up your positions; stand firm and see the deliverance the Lord will give you, Judah and Jerusalem. Do not be afraid; do not be discouraged. Go out to face them tomorrow, and the Lord will be with you."
> (2 Chronicles 20:17 NIV)

I will go out to face them tomorrow and the LORD WILL BE WITH ME!!!

I love you all very much and I thank God for you! Thank you with all my heart!!!

Love,
Lorraine (Rainie) xo

From: Lorraine
To: All
Date: October 20, 2015 1:50 PM
Subject: PS . . .

I forgot to mention that I received a wonderful email yesterday from one of our pastors asking me if I would want to be anointed with oil. I replied with a resounding YES! He said that they were having their elders meeting that evening and wanted to know if I would be able to come right before their meeting. Again, I replied YES and asked what time! Fortunately we are only a 5-minute cab ride away.

When we arrived, we were greeted by all of the elders and they asked me to share my feelings a bit. I admitted that I'm scared. They prayed over me, anointing my forehead with oil, and they asked God for His healing upon my body. I accepted it with an open heart, believing and receiving God's mercy!

> Is anyone among you sick? Let him call for the elders of the church, and let them pray over him, anointing him with oil in the name of the Lord. And the prayer of faith will save the sick, and the Lord will raise him up. And if he has committed sins, he will be forgiven. Confess your trespasses to one another, and pray for one another, that you may be healed. The effective, fervent prayer of a righteous man avails much.
> (James 5:14-16 NKJV)

I am humbled by this blessing and I thank the Lord for each of those beautiful servants of God!

9

"The Lord will
fight for you;
you need only
to be still."

EXODUS 14:14 NIV

Words That Lifted My Spirit
and Gave Me Comfort

From: Pastor Steve
To: Lorraine
Date: October 20, 2015 7:34 AM
Subject: Re:

Hi Lorraine,

I was reading the Psalms this morning and I thought of you and Greg. Take some time and read Psalms 31-37. You and Greg read them together slowly and let the Lord just bring peace to your hearts through His promises.

Steve

From: Kate
To: Lorraine
Date: October 20, 2015 2:39 PM
Subject: Re:

Hi Lorraine,

I was thinking of you this morning on my drive into work. Just breaking between sessions and caught your email. You are in my prayers, precious friend. God's loving arms are around you and holding you tight.

Much Love and healing Light to you . . .

xo,
-Kate

From: Julie A
To: Lorraine
Date: October 20, 2015 2:40 PM
Subject: Re:

Dear Lorraine,

Thanks for writing with an update. Just as surely as I share your sorrow and pain, I stand with you on God's firm foundation and His many promises of immeasurable goodness in the lives of His children. How firm a foundation it is. What a joy to see you calling upon the name of the Lord through this. Yes, our never-changing, ever-faithful God will be with you tomorrow and always! Hallelujah.

I am here for you no matter what you need, just a phone call, an email, or simply a text away. I can be at your house in 15 minutes to cook, deliver a meal, drive

11

you to chemo, read scripture, or just kvetch. If it's alone time you need, you got it. Just whatever. Anything. When you find out the nutritional guidelines, limitations, recommendations, let me know. And even if you can't eat a certain something that Greg has a hankering for, I'm happy to do that too. But generally I do healthy cooking, like homemade soups, etc.

I will be praying every day, my sister! Wisdom and skill for the doctors and nurses. For your body to respond the right way to the absolute max, and for comfort and peace through the days and weeks. God love you and lift you up in His almighty arms.

Julie xoxo

From: Sandy R
To: Lorraine
Date: October 20, 2015 2:41 PM
Subject: Re:

Nothing to say, Lorraine. . . . Just holy silence . . . inspired by your words & praying . . .

Love you . . .

From: Susie
To: Lorraine
Date: October 20, 2015 4:40 PM
Subject: Re:

Rainie,

I haven't been able to get you off my mind. I was hoping & praying just like you that a new doctor may have found different results and I am so sorry you didn't get better news. I will be thinking of you tomorrow, sweet girl, and in all the days to come. I won't stop praying for you, "I promise." I am also hoping that your chemo treatments will be tolerable and not make you too sick or weak. I love you so much, Rainie, and have always looked up to you. You, "Cool Cousin," have left a lasting lifetime impression on all your younger and less cool cousins. ;)

I feel like you are one of God's little angels here on earth. He's not ready for you yet. He's got big plans for you!! All my love and please send my love to Greg, as I know he must be a wreck. Please pass along my cell phone # to him so that if he needs me for you for any reason, I'll be there.

Love you,
Susie

From: Phyllis
To: Lorraine
Date: October 20, 2015 7:15 PM
Subject: Re:

Lorraine, thinking about you today . . .

In **Matthew 21:21-22** (NASB) it says, "And Jesus answered and said to them, 'Truly I say to you, if you have faith and do not doubt, you will not only do what was done to the fig tree, but even if you say to this mountain, 'Be taken up and cast into the sea,' it will happen. 'And all things you ask in prayer, believing, you will receive.'"

I believe that FAITH makes MIRACLES, even though the circumstances and diagnoses given seem daunting. It should never be in our hearts to feel daunted, scared, unable, or unwilling to believe God. So we must trust. We must pray. We must believe. We serve a God that is sooooo BIG, and who is still in the business of doing miracles today, so I'm leaving my fears at His feet and praying real hard.

Love you,
Phyllis

From: Mariellen
To: Lorraine
Date: October 20, 2015 8:22 PM
Subject: Re:

Lorraine,

I think you are wise to have secured other opinions and to take this course of action to attack the cancer! It is shocking that it came back, but you are strong and God will give you everything you need to face each day and each treatment. We are here to love and support you through this fight. We will fight alongside of you in prayer. God will go before you and behind you, and His angel armies will protect you.

We will be praying throughout the day tomorrow that your body will receive the treatment well with no adverse reactions. We are praying for the wisdom and perfect execution of each step of your treatment, and for the sensitivity, awareness, and intellectual excellence of each member of your medical team. Most of all we are praying for God to stand beside you through your day and for His presence to give you strength, peace, comfort, and health.

No need is too big or small. Once you know what the treatments will be like and what you will need, let us know and we will make it happen.

We love you and stand on the Lord's promise:

> "So do not fear, for I am with you; do not be dismayed, for I am your God. I will strengthen you and help you; I will uphold you with my righteous right hand."
> (Isaiah 41:10 NIV)

We will get through this, beautiful friend, and we will celebrate your victory together!

Love,
Mariellen & Garen

From: Beth
To: Lorraine
Date: October 21, 2015 4:28 AM
Subject: Re:

Dear, sweet, lovely Rainie,

I'm awake and praying so hard for you. I know you will handle whatever comes your way with faith and grace.

I love you so much,
Beth

From: Christina
To: Lorraine
Date: October 21, 2015, 2:14 PM
Subject: Re:

Aunt Rainie,

I was so shocked to hear the news. I'm so sorry. You are strong and you will get through this. You have all of us supporting you and praying for you. Keep us updated on your treatments and let us know if you need anything. You are always in our thoughts and prayers!

Love,
Christina

From: Elsa
To: Lorraine
Date: October 21, 2015 3:32 PM
Subject: Re:

Hi Lorraine,

I just wanted to let you know that I am praying for you. I pray that today went well and that you are getting some rest right now. This will be a journey, and you are so right in claiming the promises of God that He has given in His Word. I pray that as you see Him more clearly through this time of turbulence, you will be changed into His likeness. That is where the true relief and peace will come from. My prayer is of course for your physical strength and healing, but also that your soul and heart will be nourished by Christ Himself. "For from him and through him and to him are all things" (Romans 11:36 ESV).

Love you too,
Elsa

From: Harry
To: Lorraine
Date: October 20, 2015 9:22 PM
Subject: Re:

Lorraine . . .

In reflecting on this today, I couldn't help but think about a child and a father in the midst of a raging storm. That child would never have the opportunity to experience the full spectrum of comfort from his father and closeness to his father apart from that storm. Then in the light of day and in the warmth of the sun, he will know more than any of his peers that he has a father he can completely trust and fully depend on.

My prayer is that as you go forward in faith and resolve, you will feel your Father's hand firmly holding yours. And when you both walk into the light of day and warmth of the sun, you will know you have a Father you can completely trust and fully depend on.

Prayers going up for you, Lorraine!
Harry

From: Suzanne
To: Lorraine
Date: October 20, 2015 9:53 PM
Subject: Re:

I read in your email that you were having chemo today. I pray it went well and you won't suffer side effects. I know that the Psalms helped me through those dark days when I thought there was no more hope to my life. My mom had 3 separate bouts with cancer between age 50 and 60. She turned 81 this year. She speaks at Christian women's clubs to this day about her faith and perseverance. Even her doctors said she only had a 50/50 chance of surviving the first year. She just felt God would heal her and lived that way from that day on. She has had no reoccurrence for the last 20 years. She uses a lot of holistic advice when it comes to nutrition, as do you. Her doctors said they thought she rebounded so quickly because of her good health.

God in his goodness knows our days, our hairs on our head, and promises to be with us always. I have had to rely on that and that only. I pray that your chemo goes smoothly, with as few side effects as possible with no reoccurrence. When you feel better, I would love to get together. Even for a short lunch downtown. Know you are in my prayers.

Suzanne

From: Teresa
To: Lorraine
Date: October 20, 2015 10:20 PM
Subject: Re:

Beautiful Lorraine . . . Rainie . . .

You are lovely, beautiful, and tenacious. I'm sitting here after reading your email, and I ask the Lord, "Father, I'm tempted to ask You, 'Why?'" Instead I will declare: "God! You are God. Is this report too difficult for You? I know my God and nothing is too hard for You."

I'm thanking God for having already made a way, and, Father, I am thanking You in advance for a miracle beyond our wildest dreams over Lorraine and Greg. As Lorraine has believed in You for others and has even seen You come through, so I declare what she has been able to witness You do for others that, Lord, You will do for her! Holy Spirit, thank You for Your reminders that the name of Jesus is above every name. Holy Spirit, thank You for Your Spirit of Wisdom and Understanding, Counsel, Might, and Knowledge and the fear of the Lord coming to rest on everyone involved and that our fears be silenced, severed, and sent to Jesus, who will do with it what He does, and let us see

Lorraine live and declare the works of the Lord! We call forth the accelerated DNA of Jesus to stop any acceleration of this reported diagnosis in Jesus's name!!!!! God! Show up and show out in Jesus's name!!!!!!

Love you so much!!!
Teresa

The Power of Words!

Peace came over me again and again as I read through each email. There were many more . . . more than I have room for in this book! Believe me, though—they are all in my journal and I will keep them with me always, to give thanks to God for each loving person and be reminded of His unmerited favor over my life, as He has blessed me with the most incredible, loving friends and family! I'm humbled and I'm grateful!

CHAPTER 4

Week #1 Had Arrived

I awakened to a warm October morning and a magnificent sunrise. I felt at peace. I was greeted by a beautiful letter of love and encouragement from my husband and a prayer of protection over me for the day. He would be leaving work early and meeting me at the hospital before the start of my treatment. I had multiple texts from loving friends, including a photo of the sunrise and a scripture verse from my friend Maria, and a message from my dear friend Carol, who had included a photo of a large bell hanging in her backyard. This bell is a symbol to her and a tangible way to touch the hearts of those in need across the miles. She went on to pray for me and ring this bell every single week of treatment! That first treatment morning she said, "I just rang the bell for you, my friend!" I can't explain the power this had for me, as I imagined her soft hand reaching out to touch me through the musical tone of this bell with its powerful call on my behalf to heaven, brought forth on the wings of angels coming to my aid at the sound.

After a light breakfast I dressed in comfortable clothing and headed to the oncology suite at the hospital. I walked the four blocks by myself—well, not really by myself. I had been texting back and forth with my prayer warrior girlfriends who surrounded me with love and encouragement. In less than an hour my veins would be injected with chemo, but first these faithful women were injecting strength into my spirit.

The waiting room is never a comfortable place to be. Especially that day. I sat there, not knowing what to expect. I looked around to see different expressions on the faces in the very crowded room, and I wondered what their day looked like. I had sent out an email to everyone who was praying for me, so I felt like I had an army of companions with me in spirit.

Seated near the lab where I would have all necessary blood work drawn, I continued to pray for protection and healing. I looked up to see a woman being led through the entrance of the lab. Her gait was unsteady. Her head was completely bald, with no eyebrows and no eyelashes, and her face was pale, but her complexion was clear and smooth. She was beautiful. I wondered if I would see myself as beautiful in the same way I saw this stranger. I tried not to stare at her. I tried to look away, wanting to erase that image from my mind, but as she passed, the clicking of her shoes drew my attention back to her. She walked with a bit of a limp. I wondered just what she was going through and what her prognosis was. I prayed for her, then I texted my girlfriends and asked them to join me. We prayed via text for this woman. Then I prayed a silent prayer of my own for every person in that room.

The pager they'd given me began to buzz, and I was called in for my blood work. No turning back now!

I entered the lab and was greeted by a lovely, compassionate young woman. She said she would pray for me! I received that with the most grateful heart! A nursing aide stood by to escort me to my treatment room. As I walked with her, I recalled an email from my precious friend Pam:

From: Pam
To: Lorraine
Date: October 21, 2015 5:58 AM
Subject: xoxoxoxoxoxoxxo

Praying and fasting for you today, girlfriend!

I wanted to send you this link. It was on yesterday and it was sweet and calming—about a man who has cancer and when he went in for his chemo treatments how his room (according to the nurses) was the "most peaceful" and beautiful room in the cancer ward, because he let God in and God was with him and right there!

You can be assured God is right here thru this. xoxoxo
Pam

That was just the shot in the arm (pun intended) I needed! I relied greatly on all of the encouragement I received throughout the process. These emails, texts, phone messages, etc., were powerful. The words and prayers of these loving people gave me strength and peace every step of the way. I'm including some of them in this book to say that if you know someone going through a serious challenge, this type of encouragement is just what they need to help them forge ahead!

I printed out several emails to read throughout that first day of treatment because I needed to read those words again. I held them tightly against my chest as we journeyed down the long hallway to my treatment room, possibly to calm my rapidly beating heart.

The room I was given had a stunning lake view. I sat on the bed and tried to silence the thoughts in my head and enjoy the view, but I couldn't. A lovely nurse entered and spoke gently to calm me as she inserted my first IV and started the pre-meds (Benadryl, a steroid, and an anti-nausea drug).

I needed to read a few more emails, so I paged through them and started with my dear friend Jaime at the top of the stack:

From: Jaime
To: Lorraine
Date: October 20, 2015 10:03 AM
Subject: morning encouragement

Sweet Bella Lorraine, not a day goes by that you are not in our conversation, in our thoughts, in our prayers. This morning's encouragement:

 This is the confidence we have in approaching God: that if we ask anything according to his will, he hears us. And if we know that he hears us—whatever we ask—we know that we have what we asked of him.
(1 John 5:14-15 NIV)

I am standing by your side agreeing DAILY with you for your healing!!! I only wish I could be there in person to be a help, but I am so thankful God has placed so many willing people in your path that are ready to stop in, bring a meal, do some laundry, whatever it may be!!! My prayers will not cease. I believe His hand is upon you and that healing is YOURS!!!! We're with you, Bella, we're with you!!!!

Feeling fired up ~ sending you hugs and all our love,
xoxoxo j

Time was going quickly. After reading only one email, my eyes became heavy and I felt myself being forced by the Benadryl to relax. I fought it. I wanted to stay alert and see what was going on at least until my husband arrived. It was noon and the chemo was scheduled to start at about the same time he would get there.

My phone kept buzzing with texts from my dear prayer warrior girl-friends. As I tried to text, my fingers wouldn't cooperate and the amount of typos was increasing, so I began to dictate. I could hear myself slurring a bit, and it was obvious the phone couldn't understand me. The texts were making little to no sense. I began to giggle with every mistake! Greg arrived early and walked into my room to find me talking into my phone and laughing. When I saw the look on his face, my giggles turned to belly laughter and I could not stop! At one point I told him (in my slurred speech), "I'm the funniest person I've ever met!" The nurse walked in to check on me and to introduce herself to Greg. I could see that she was pleased to find that I was no longer focused on the needle in my arm! As she prepared to administer my first round of chemo, I was in very good spirits!

Chemo bag #1 lasted about an hour, followed by a second bag (a different chemo drug) for another hour. The time went quickly and without a problem. The long treatment day was drawing to an end and the effects of the Benadryl were dissipating enough for me to stand on stable feet and gather my things.

We walked home slowly as I clung to the strong arm of my loving husband. All was well.

From: Lorraine
To: All
Date: October 21, 2015 9:19 PM
Subject: chemo one is done

Hi everyone!

Chemo one is done and it went well. Praise God!

I slept well last night and woke up peaceful and felt good. I walked over to the hospital with God holding my right hand. Greg got there shortly after to hold my other hand!

When I got there, they did blood work and a short exam and then some education and "pre-meds." They gave me good drugs to prevent nausea and any allergic reactions. The day went quickly. We left there at 4:00, walked home on this gorgeous day, and had dinner. I'm getting ready to go to bed right now but wanted you to know and wanted to thank you all once again for your faithful prayers and love!

Praying now that no adverse side effects will occur. The chemo stays in the body for three days, so I have to drink lots of water to flush it out. I pray for no nausea (although they gave me a prescription that should keep it away). The list of side effects is pretty extensive, but they don't happen to everyone and I pray the do not happen to me.

Everyone at the hospital was wonderful. I even had a room with a view of the lake. I sit here at home this evening looking out at the same lake at night, lit up by colorful boat lights. What wonderful, warm fall weather the boaters are having as they get to enjoy the lake awhile longer.

One silly side note: the Benadryl they gave me made me sleepy and my speech was a bit slurred. I was trying to text by dictating into my phone. I sent a couple that were pretty crazy and kept going back to try to correct them. It tickled me and I could not stop laughing! Greg and the nurses were making fun of me and of course that made me laugh harder! God is good! Laughter is truly the best medicine!

Praying for many more good . . . GREAT days!

A joyful heart is good medicine, but a broken spirit dries up the bones.
(Proverbs 17:22 NASB)

I love you all and thank you again! I felt so comforted and covered by your prayers and I feel loved. Before I got out of bed this morning, I prayed for each of you! I do every day!

The grace of the Lord Jesus Christ, and the love of God, and the fellowship of the Holy Spirit, be with you all.
(2 Corinthians 13:14 NASB)

Going to bed now. More soon . . .

*A joyful heart
is good medicine,
but a broken spirit
dries up the bones.*

PROVERBS 17:22 NASB

From: Dr. Kehoe
To: Lorraine
Date: October 21, 2015 9:23 PM
Subject: Re: Chemo one is done

Lorraine,

Thanks so much for the update. I love your attitude. Keep it up. Sleep well.

Bill

From: Teresa
To: Lorraine
Date: October 22, 2015 7:30 AM
Subject: Re: chemo one is done

I love you, Lorraine—I wish I could be there giggling with you!!! Such a beautiful daughter of the King!!

From: Pam
To: Lorraine
Date: October 21, 2015 9:43 PM
Subject: Re: chemo one is done

hi sweet angel!!! so glad your day was brighter than anticipated . . . joy and laughter are my favorite graces/mercies from the Lord. He is the Lord of Laughter! He has taught me joy in the midst of sorrows . . . still does!

xoxoxoxo
rest, angel,
Pam (Jill) ;)

From: Kim
To: Lorraine
Date: October 21, 2015 9:53 PM
Subject: Re: chemo one is done

Thank you so much for this update. I do not want to bother you with update requests, but it is so HARD not to ask for them. God gave your mom, and you, that sense of humor. It serves you (and us all) well. Rest well, Cuz . . . love you.

From: Sandy O
To: Lorraine
Date: October 21, 2015 10:21 PM
Subject: Re: chemo one is done

Sleep well in His grace and love. So glad it went well today!

From: Harry
To: Lorraine
Date: October 22, 2015 1:23 AM
Subject: Re: chemo one is done

Well, Lorraine . . . if you look at the time stamp on this email, you will see that you had a much better night's sleep than me!!! Ha-ha! I'm so glad to hear that your treatment today went better than you had anticipated. Praise the Lord for that! I know you felt the prayers of everyone. Your positive and faith-driven outlook on this adversity has really marked me. Reading your inspiring words is giving me a new outlook. You're such an example of grace and appreciation, Lorraine. God has and will continue to use you in a very mighty way as you forge ahead.

We look forward to hearing more of how God is working in this and through this! Rest well!

Harry

From: Jaime
To: Lorraine
Date: October 22, 2015 9:40 AM
Subject: Re: chemo one is done

What a joy to read your message this morning. I am laughing, picturing your talk/text scenario. Oh, Bella, what a TESTIMONY you are to every single person next to you watching you walk FEARLESSLY through this. Even if fear tries to creep up, you thwart it with bravery and courage, refusing to let anything tell you differently about who your God is and His relentless love for you!!!

I am so honored to be an eyewitness to your pilgrimage. It is building my faith in ways you do not realize, and Anthony and I are steadfast in prayer for you daily. I have not seen Anthony this emotionally attached to praying someone through a battle like this, so I know the Lord is using it to do something mighty in him too.

I love you!!!

From: Jean
To: Lorraine
Date: October 22, 2015 9:41 AM
Subject: Re: chemo one is done

I can't tell you how happy this makes me to hear it went so well. I thought of you most of yesterday and will continue to pray. Have I told you how much I love and admire you? Tears of joy fill my soul. ♡

CHAPTER 5

Chemo #2

From: Lorraine
To: All
Date: October 27, 2015, 10:29 PM
Subject: Chemo #2 tomorrow

Hi friends and family,

Chemo two is tomorrow. I have to be there at 11:40. It will be a shorter day because I have only one chemo drug tomorrow.

Please pray for another good outcome and of course, as always, no ill side effects. I'm getting ready to go to sleep now and praying for a good night's rest. I also pray that each of you sleep well!

> A tranquil heart is life to the body. . . .
> (Proverbs 14:30a NASB)

Thank you so much for keeping me in prayer!

Love,
Lorraine/Rainie

From: Dr. Kehoe
To: Lorraine
Date: October 27, 2015 10:38 PM
Subject: Re: Chemo #2 tomorrow

You are in my prayers. Tomorrow is going to be a great day!! Sleep tight!!

Bill

From: Melissa
To: Lorraine
Date: October 27, 2015 11:57 PM
Subject: Re: Chemo #2 tomorrow

You got it, sweet friend! I'm praying in hopeful expectation of the medicinal effectiveness of number 2, minus side effects. You just knock them down, one after the other, one at a time.

Many prayers and much love! Praying you are sleeping well!

Melissa xxoo

My second week began the same way as the first. I awoke to a beautiful day with a loving note and prayer from my husband and multiple emails and texts from friends and family. I was strengthened by their heartwarming words of encouragement.

I walked the same path again this week, praying and thanking God that He never leaves me. I think walking to my appointment by myself and having my husband meet me there later was good for me. It made me that much more aware of God's presence and His hand holding onto me as I placed my feet on the path set before me, marching forward in faith and recalling many of the words that lifted me and strengthened me for the journey:

From: Kathy S
To: Lorraine
Date: October 28, 2015 2:15 AM
Subject: Re: Chemo #2 tomorrow

Thankful that you walk with "the helmet of salvation, and the sword of the Spirit, which is the word of God" [Ephesians 6:17 KJV]. Your body is His temple.

I love you, Kathy

From: Kate
To: Lorraine
Date: October 28, 2015 7:11 AM
Subject: Re: Chemo #2 tomorrow

Praying for continued strength . . . and peace that you feel God's presence with you every step of the way . . .

Much Love & Hugs to you . . . xo, Kate

From: Pastor Steve
To: Lorraine
Date: October 28, 2015 8:44 AM
Subject: Re: Chemo #2 tomorrow

Just letting you know I was praying for you this morning before seeing this.

Steve

From: Lorraine
To: All
Date: October 28, 2015 4:40 PM
Subject: Chemo #2 is through!

I walked there again this morning, hand in hand with the Lord. Chemo went well. I didn't feel anything except drowsiness from the Benadryl, and of course that didn't last long. Afterwards Greg and I walked home arm in arm, relaxed, and had nice comfort meal.

> You make known to me the path of life; you will fill me with joy in your presence, with eternal pleasures at your right hand. (Psalm 16:11 NIV)

God blessed the day in countless ways, big and small! As I was leaving our building, I saw our doorman. He knows about my situation. He has a heart of compassion. I asked him if he was responsible for a lovely flower arrangement I received from the building with a heartwarming note. He said, "I'm not at liberty to say." ;) I gave him a hug and told him I was on my way to chemo 2. As I turned to wave to him again, I noticed a tender look of concern on his face, and with his hands placed together, he said, "I'm praying." The beautiful skies I awoke to this morning had turned drizzly and windy, but as I walked out the door, the rain stopped and I didn't need to open my umbrella. Sweet blessings.

When I arrived at the hospital, I met some lovely people in the waiting room. So many different stories sitting in that room. I wondered what each one was facing . . . thinking . . . feeling. I prayed silently for them. When I was escorted to the chemo treatment area, it was crowded. There are way too many people in this world facing cancer right now! Way too many!!! The crowded room had only one chair available at the time we entered. I was glad when they walked me back to a little private room with a door and a nice big easy chair and another chair for Greg to sit in when he arrived—another sweet blessing. I settled in and relaxed in my chair while I waited for all the blood test results to come back, and I prayed for every single person in that place! I prayed for healing, for comfort, for the love of God to fill their hearts and for peace . . . real peace . . . the peace that only comes from the God of all comfort—the one who made us and knows every detail of our being, down to the number of hairs on our heads . . . and the exact number of hairs each of those patients has lost and the number that will grow back! This is the God who made us! This is the God who loves us! Nothing can separate us from this Love. All we have to do is receive it! I prayed!!! And I pray!!!

 "The Lord turn his face toward you and give you peace."
(Numbers 6:26 NIV)

Thank you as always for your faithful prayers! You remain in mine!

Love,
Lorraine/Rainie

From: Kathy S
To: Lorraine
Date: October 28, 2015 11:18 PM
Subject: Chemo #2 is through!

Oh Lorraine! You are so beautiful. So filled with God's love. Thank you for sharing your day's experiences. I wept as I read because you touched me deeply.

Thank you . . . and I thank God . . . Two Is Through!!!

From: Susie
To: Lorraine
Date: October 29, 2015 3:46 PM
Subject: Re: Chemo #2 is through!

Hi Rainie,

I am relieved beyond words that you are responding so well to your treatments. I sure hope that this is a continued pattern for you the entire 18 weeks. It does seem like they have come a long way with treating the adverse side effects that go along with the territory. Too bad they can't come up with one that won't make you lose your hair. But again, you have already gone wig shopping, so you are prepared. You are a little trooper. Honestly . . . do you ever allow yourself to feel bad or disgusted, frustrated and just mad? I think it is only human nature to feel those emotions??

Only curious because I already think you're pretty perfect. Ha-ha, oh my goodness, if you only knew the pedestal we had you on when we were young. I think you're still up there. LOL—don't fall off, Rainie . . . just keep waving and smiling from your pedestal.

Love you,
Sus

From: Lorraine
To: Susie
Date: October 29, 2015 4:48 PM
Subject: Re: Re: Chemo #2 is through!

You are so cute, Susie!!

Of course I feel frustrated, angry, etc. I've got my parents' spunk combined with their humor ;) . . . but the Word of God is teaching me so much about handling my emotions properly and it puts life into the right perspective when we stay in His Word. There is so much wisdom there. It comes straight from Him to us. It's our relationship with Him that gives us strength. For me, it takes discipline and the study of the Bible continually. It isn't something that is instant. It's not from my work or my own strength . . . but from His. As for fear . . . it is the opposite of faith. We are wired up to love, but we learn to fear. I also learned from a book by Dr. Carolyn Leaf that according to research, 75–98% of mental and physical illness comes from toxic thoughts. Stress is an enemy, Sus!

Anyway . . . yes, I'm human . . . not superwoman. Even though you want me to be. ;) Well, I guess I can say I'm a princess, though. Daughter of the King Most High! I'll wear my tiara with my wig and keep waving and smiling from my pedestal. LOL

Love you so much, Sus!
Rainie xoxo

"The Lord turn his face toward you and give you peace."

NUMBERS 6:26 NIV

From: Dr. Kehoe
To: Lorraine
Date: October 29, 2015 11:02 AM
Subject: Re: Chemo #2 is through!

Please keep me on your email list. They are precious. I love your attitude.

Bill

From: Pastor Steve
To: Lorraine
Date: October 29, 2015 11:43 AM
Subject: Re: Chemo #2 is through!

Lorraine and Greg, again we prayed for you this morning, and, Lorraine, let me encourage you to be keeping a journal, if you aren't already. These emails are a real blessing.

Steve

CHAPTER 6

Chemo #3 — Went Speedily!

From: Lorraine
To: All
Date: November 3, 2015 8:20 PM
Subject: Chemo 3 is tomorrow

Hi all!

I had a good week and felt normal. Praise God! Tomorrow is chemo #3. Boy that week flew by! I realize I've already told you, but I'm grateful for your faithful prayers!

Love,
Lorraine/Rainie

From: Laura D
To: Lorraine
Date: November 3, 2015 10:01 PM
Subject: Re: Chemo 3 is tomorrow

Hello my friend,

I love you and I'm praying for you today.

From: Phyllis
To: Lorraine
Date: November 3, 2015 8:26 PM
Subject: Re: Chemo 3 is tomorrow

Lorraine,

I am so thankful that our prayers are being answered. Hoping chemo #3 continues to go well.

Sending lots of hugs to go with more prayers,

Phyllis

From: Dr. Kehoe
To: Lorraine
Date: November 3, 2015 9:00 PM
Subject: Re: Chemo 3 is tomorrow

Lorraine,

Keep on going!! Sounds like you're tolerating the chemo well! You have lots of support.

Bill

From: Jaime
To: Lorraine
Date: November 4, 2015 11:55 AM
Subject: Re: Chemo 3 is tomorrow

That week DID fly by!!! And not a moment of it were you not in our hearts, our thoughts, our prayers . . . remaining steadfast with you. Love you so much, my Princess Warrior, my inspiration, my sister for life.

xoxoxo j

From: Kathy S
To: Lorraine
Date: November 5, 2015 6:27 AM
Subject: Chemo 3 is tomorrow

Sweet Lorraine,

Thank you for sharing your journey as you walk with our Lord with a childlike faith. You are His daughter! He loves you and is loving others through you!

I love you!

Kathy

From: Lorraine
To: ALL
Date: November 5, 2015 3:53 PM
Subject: Chemo 3 went speedily

Hi friends and family!

Chemo 3 really did go speedily! And I'm so glad! It was just one drug again this week. The room was not crowded this time.

They got me in from the waiting room for my blood work right away and into the infusion area on time. They started the IV drip with saline and pre-meds and then the chemo. By the time Greg arrived, I was about 5 minutes away from being finished. I had one of my favorite nurses today. It gave me peace. Sometimes a certain nurse will have a certain level of compassion or a personality that is better suited to my own. She was my nurse the first day when the Benadryl made me laugh and she encouraged that laughter. She even got all of Greg's silly jokes! ;) We had fun together. The joy of the Lord is our strength!!!

While waiting to be called in this week, a woman who seemed to be running late for her appointment was rushing in as someone was directing her where to go. She was bald and laboring to breathe with every step. I prayed for her, and then I sent a quick text to some of my prayer warriors who are always on standby and I asked them to join me in prayer for her breathing and for God's intervention in whatever she is dealing with and that she might feel His presence like a warm blanket over her. They immediately started texting back: "I'm praying for this woman right now" . . . "I just prayed for her" . . . "I'm lifting her up to the Lord, this woman who God knows intimately" . . . "I lift her up to Him right now." It was two or more of us joined in prayer for a precious child of God. I keep thinking about her, as the image of her walking past me brought her to my attention in that waiting room. I pray for her still.

I think about the saying:

"I cried because I had no shoes; then I met a man who had no feet."

God knows exactly where we are. Nothing escapes Him. Nothing is too small or too large for Him to handle. He is able . . . more than able! He is with us and loves us beyond our comprehension and we can trust Him.

Oh, I had another sweet blessing from someone in my building. Two in fact this week. I met a woman who is going through breast cancer treatment . . . taking tamoxifen for stage 1 breast cancer and doing well. My doorman introduced us and we've become friends. We took a long walk together Tuesday. She is such a beautiful, kind woman, and it was a wonderful way to take advantage of a glorious day! If you remember, please pray for Maria.

Also, a lovely woman who cleans for the building has been encouraging me in special ways. She sends me information and talks to me in the lobby whenever we see each other and gives me giant hugs. The night before last, I had a message from the front desk that Carmy had something for me. The doorman paged her to tell her I was back home, and the next thing I knew, I heard a small tap on our door. The first thing out of her mouth when I opened the door was, "I love you." She's a prayer warrior too . . . with a heart of gold. She wanted to share a healthy recipe with me. How sweet is that! I thank God for Carmy! I love her too!

Blessings are all around us. If we just look, we can see them.

Praying for a good weekend . . . symptom free! Next Wednesday will be my long day. 8:00 for blood work; 8:30 for my doctor visit and exam; 9:00 for chemo. I'll have both chemo drugs next week. Praying for a good outcome and no ill side effects, as always.

Thank you again for being here for me! You know I appreciate every prayer and every act of love!!!

Love to you all and God bless you!
Lorraine/Rainie

From: Dr. Kehoe
To: Lorraine
Date: November 5, 2015 6:57 PM
Subject: Re: Chemo 3 went speedily

Lorraine,

I love your thoughts and your faith. Your story is inspirational to all who know you!

Bill

From: Sandy O
To: Lorraine
Date: November 5, 2015 7:04 PM
Subject: Re: Chemo 3 went speedily

Hi Lorraine!

So glad #3 went well! God is blessing you with being able to see people and their situations through eyes of love. That is a wonderful gift from Him. Will join you in praying for a good, symptom-free weekend.

Love you! Sandy

From: Debby
To: Lorraine
Date: November 6, 2015 2:37 PM
Subject: Re: Chemo 3 went speedily

It's beautiful how God can be seen in every detail. For whatever reason we go through the trials, and for whatever reason God doesn't take the trial away, it's always for the good. In your case I can't help but think that all these people you're meeting are in need of comfort and understanding, and God could have chosen anyone to be that source of strength to them, but He chose you.

Love,
Debby

CHAPTER 7

A Woman's Crowning Glory

I just mentioned the woman with no hair in the last chapter. And just as I wondered how I would feel once presented with the side effect of hair loss, I awoke to that reality.

The nurses—as well as my precious friend Carol, who had also gone through cancer treatment—told me that it is usually right after week three when the hair begins to come out very quickly. It was about halfway between week three and four—a Friday morning. I woke up and sat at the edge of the bed and began to run my fingers through my hair, only to find myself holding a clump of hair the size of a bird's nest in the palms of both of my hands.

I recalled one of the many phone conversations I'd had with Carol, when she shared so many helpful tips with me. She advised me to take control and have my head shaved before it started falling out. She said that she did this during her treatment, and she felt empowered. She refused to let it get to her, and she would not see herself as a victim. She said, "I never wanted anyone to think of me as sick. I wasn't sick." She suggested that I find some great wigs and have fun experimenting with different looks. Carol told me that she bought herself three wigs: one black, one red, and one brunette. She said, "I would wake up each morning and decide which color and style hair I wanted to have that day." Carol sported those wigs with class! She always wore her best clothes, jewelry, and makeup, and carried herself with confidence. She was and is victorious! She has been cancer free since 2010! I'm so thankful for her good health. I'm also grateful for the way she walked with me through chemo from beginning to end! She blessed me in countless ways!

As soon as my hair started falling out, I took Carol's advice and contacted my hairdresser immediately. When I called to find out if he could squeeze me in for a "head shave," his wife informed me that he was out of town but assured me that she would have him contact me when he returned. A few days went by and I was beginning to think that I might not hear from him. I told my husband, "I don't care who shaves my head. I just want to get this over with. I think I might just go to a barbershop!" Just as I said this, the phone rang. It was Anthony, my hairdresser. He apologized for the delay in getting back to me and explained that he was out of town and had just returned the night before. He said he would be happy to help me and asked if I could come in Saturday late in the day so that the salon would not be crowded and so that we could have a bit more privacy. I gratefully accepted his invitation.

Greg wanted to go with me for support. I was so glad! He and I arrived at Anthony's salon at 5:00, just before closing. Anthony escorted us to his section, where he sat and talked to us for a bit before we started. He spoke with such a gentle tone as he explained what he was about to do. He also listened intently when I expressed my concerns. Anthony said he wanted to take this in stages . . . meaning that he would cut my hair a little at a time, revealing several haircuts in one sitting. I told him that wasn't necessary: "Just chop off the ponytail and shave the rest. I'm fine . . . really. I'm fine with this."

He gently smiled and said, "If you will allow, I really prefer to do this in stages. In fact, as we do, I think you just might be convinced that short hair is beautiful on you."

Greg and I looked at each other with amazement that this man had such compassion and concern for my emotional adjustment to what was about to take place. I agreed and settled in to his chair with confidence. In fact I already had confidence in Anthony. He is the best! His experience spans the globe, and he has actually styled the hair of many famous people. Of course I wasn't looking for a style . . . just a solution to this problem, freeing me to move ahead, but Anthony offered much more than that. He handled those tools with such a flare and without an ounce of show—just humility in using the gift he has been given to bless me (and so many others)!

After the first cut my hair was just above my shoulders—in a sassy, layered bob . . . very cute. Anthony told me to just relax and that he would be back in a minute. He walked away. We quickly found out that this was his way of giving me time to adjust to each change—every cut being a high-style look that anyone would be happy to pay for and wear with pride! He continued this process of cutting and then walking away, all the way through four different styles. Greg was in awe of Anthony's expertise, feeling as though he was watching a true master at work. He was also loving the different looks and encouraged me to remember these going forward. He said, "I think you are going to be a short-hair person after this!" Not ever having had short hair, I gave him a look of doubt, yet at the same time I continued to admire each new look.

My hair colorist, Becky, was there with us the entire time as well. She had decided not to go home at the end of her shift. She said she wanted to stay with me and with us. Becky was a beautiful encouragement to me throughout as she cheered me on, and assured me that she would be praying for me on the road ahead. She believed with us that God would not leave my side but would lead me step by step to victory.

After the final cut Anthony asked us to move to a more private area, where he would then use the electric razor to buzz the remaining hair. He even placed the razor in my hand so that I could feel the sensation about to take place on my head. I was still confident and ready. Then the buzz of the razor removed all but about an inch around my entire head, with just a bit more left on top. He stopped there and said that this would enable the rest to gradually and evenly come out without being noticeable. He kept saying,

"You are beautiful."

Then he and Becky said in unison, "You have a great shaped head." LOL! I replied, "I don't think I've ever received such a compliment before, so thank you." ;)

The cut was finished, but Anthony wasn't. Even though we had been there for almost two and half hours, he asked if I'd brought my wig. I did.

He asked, "May I style it for you?" I gratefully agreed! After styling my wig he placed it on my head so that I could walk out with confidence. My shoulder-length, layered wig was a pretty color of highlighted blonde—a color I never thought I would wear. I remembered Carol's comments about trying something different. This was a new look for me, and I was ready to show the world!

Before we left, Greg and I continued to thank Anthony for this amazing experience, and to thank Becky for her selfless companionship. When it came time to pay, we were deeply touched as Anthony insisted we receive this as his gift to me. Greg could not hold back the tears as he said, "I can never repay you for the beautiful way you have blessed my wife. You have taken her from one place to another so gently and kindly. It was amazing to watch the dance between the two of you as you both moved through this emotional experience. Thank you for using your talents and for being so kind to my wife!"

There were really no more words to utter. The four of us huddled together in a circle, hugging and crying. Yes, all four of us. When the tears dried, we all agreed that we were blessed to have this time led by God, and to feel His love so powerfully!

As we made our way to the door, we paused, turned to wave a final good-bye, and then I blew them a kiss, tapped my hand against my heart, and did a quick curtsy in my new blonde do!

I did walk with confidence and I did plan to have fun with the new looks—and just as Carol said: I'm not sick! I'm not a victim! I'm victorious! I'm also very aware of how blessed I am to have been graced with such amazing people who have touched my life with such generosity, exposing the enormity of their loving hearts!

God is so kind . . . so gracious . . . so compassionate.

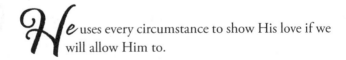
He uses every circumstance to show His love if we will allow Him to.

CHAPTER 8

Chemo #4

From: Lorraine
To: All
Date: November 10, 2015 9:00 PM
Subject: Chemo 4 tomorrow

Chemo #4 is tomorrow. It will be a long day. I have to be there at 8 a.m. so I'd better get to bed right now! Two chemo drugs, with my doctor exam first. Praying for good, sweet sleep tonight and another good outcome, as always! Thanks so much for your prayers!

Love,
Lorraine/Rainie

From: Dr. Kehoe
To: Lorraine
Date: November 10, 2015 9:48 PM
Subject: Re: Chemo 4 tomorrow

Sleep well! You will do fine. No worries!

From: Shannon
To: Lorraine
Date: November 10, 2015 11:21 PM
Subject: Re: Chemo 4 tomorrow

Sweet Dreams, Princess Rainie! ☺

I'm still praying for you daily. Sending you love and hugs. Xoxo

From: Kathy S
To: Lorraine
Date: November 11, 2015 7:45 AM
Subject: Re: Chemo 4 tomorrow

You are covered by the ONE who hears our prayers.

From: Nancy H
To: Lorraine
Date: November 11, 2015 7:50 AM
Subject: Re: chemo 4 tomorrow

Hi Lorraine,

Thinking of you and your two-drug regimen. I like this verse:

 "On the day I called, you answered me; my strength of soul you increased" [Psalm 138: 3 ESV].

You'll do fine. I know it!

Love,
Nancy and Jack

From: Julie A
To: Lorraine
Date: November 10, 2015 9:46 PM
Subject: Re: Chemo 4 tomorrow

Dear Lorraine,

I always pray for you and will be tomorrow too. Funny thing, of all the emails I get, yours is by far the most uplifting and inspirational. You have a keen sense of gratitude and joy that most people don't have, even and maybe especially in your trial.

I know God will sustain you tomorrow and for the 14 weeks after tomorrow. Soon you'll be on the road to recovery—actually you are now. By taking these difficult steps you've turned your situation around and are headed in a positive direction. Thank you for sharing your journey with your friends; we are blessed by you.

Sending love and prayers and good thoughts for tomorrow! Julie

CHAPTER 9

Chemo #5 — Tomorrow and a Short Update

From: Lorraine
To: All
Date: November 16, 2015 9:26 PM
Subject: Chemo 5 and a short update

Hi friends and family!

I have been trying to sit down to write an update all week. It's been a busy few days. As you know, this was my long day with two different chemo drugs. I had an allergic reaction to my first chemo drug (Taxol). They say that if you don't react to Taxol by now, then you should not react. But I did . . . "Well, aren't I special!" The reaction I had made my head feel like it was on fire and my face turned beet red. I knew it was bad by the wide-eyed look on the nurse's face. I was so startled that all I could do was exclaim (and loudly), "Jesus!" The nurse stopped the drip immediately and administered a heavy-duty anti-allergy drug. Within a few moments all was back to normal and I was able to complete my treatment. If it wasn't for that, it would have been a great day.

Actually it was a great day. I felt the protection of God in that room! There were many blessings throughout the day. Our cousin, Missy, came with me. She was an excellent advocate and was able to take great notes during the doctor's exam and watch over me all day until Greg arrived. It was comforting to have her with me. Also, I got my CA125 [a blood marker for cancer] back today and it came down quite a bit. It's still high, but as we know, these are just trends, and since it came down, this is a sign the chemo is working! Praise God!

Please keep the prayers going . . . specifically for no more reactions and NO side effects. Also that my veins be protected from the IVs. They did irritate two of my veins, which have become red and tender. The first one healed already from week two. The doctor said it is phlebitis (basically an irritation or inflammation of the veins). He is not overly concerned, but it's something to keep an eye on.

Oh . . . a silly side note: those steroids had me so hyper. I had an appointment with another doctor on the following day after my treatment. I had to pick Greg up from work and drive to the appointment. He says that I was driving a bit quickly and telling everyone else how to drive. He asked me to PLEASE pull over and let him drive. I kept saying, "No, I'm just fine and there is no safe place to pull this car over. Just relax and stop being so hyper!" LOL, what a hoot! Greg made sure to take the car key from me when we got to the appointment. He insisted on driving back home. I said, "I'm fine with that. I'd rather sit quietly in the passenger seat." On the way home he did have to remind me a couple of times that I had promised to sit quietly. ;)

Chemo 5 is tomorrow. I will certainly update you more afterwards. Thank you so much, beautiful friends and family, for standing with me in prayer. I'm deeply touched by the loving-kindness shown to me. I hope you continue to enjoy the nice days we are having. It really has been a glorious fall this year!

Love,
Lorraine/Rainie xoxo

From: Debby
To: Lorraine
Date: November 17, 2015 9:01 AM
Subject: Re: Chemo 5 and a short update

Dear Lorraine,

Thinking of and praying for you. Thank you for the updates. I pray that you are enveloped in God's peace in every minute and second of your day and that the drip encounters no resistance or allergic reactions—that the procedure will go quickly and without a hitch.

Love you, Sis!

PS:

 The generous will prosper; those who refresh others will themselves be refreshed.
(Proverbs 11:25 NLT)

The blessings and love you offer to other patients you meet will be returned 100 fold to you.

From: Patricia
To: Lorraine
Date: November 17, 2015 11:18 AM
Subject: Re: Chemo 5 and a short update

Lorraine,

I continue to pray for you—thank you for sharing your encouraging words. I have sent them on to several of my friends that are in "BATTLE" both physically and mentally with this illness. I pray your words will give comfort and strength and bring our God stronger into their souls. I pray God continues to be with YOU.

In His name,
Patricia

As I assemble this journal and I read once again these notes from loving friends, tears flow. I'm so grateful for the support and the love I received and the beauty of each person who wrote from their hearts such words of faith and power and strength.

CHAPTER 10

Directly from God

The following email came from my friend Teresa. We met while blogging and quickly became friends across the miles and kindred spirits—sisters in Christ. I believe this note from her was prophetic! Directly from God!

From: Teresa
To: Lorraine
Date: November 18, 2015 7:52 AM
Subject: Good Morning, Beautiful

Good morning, beautiful daughter of the King! I'm sitting here in our front living room as the sun softly peers through the windows as if it were to say, "Good morning! I must declare the glory of God. Will you join me?"

I'm writing you to let you know how the Father adores you, Lorraine. I know it seems so random to receive this email, but last night I was setting up for Christmas in the front living room, beginning to put every beautiful decoration in its proper place and SUDDENLY I saw your BEAUTIFUL face. I saw a vision of you looking through a moonlit window, as I could see both your face and your reflection in the large window that overlooked what seemed like a body of water that gracefully moved about as small waves tossed into each other with such rhythm and peace.

"With long life you shall be satisfied" are the words I saw. Immediately I was reminded of Psalm 91: "He will call on me, and I will answer him; I will be with him in trouble, I will deliver him and honor him. With long life will I satisfy him, and show him my salvation" [Psalm 91:15-16 NIV].

You are a blessing, Lorraine, and although I've never embraced you in person, I have countless times in the "spirit!" I wish I could sit with you and just visit with you and hear the boundless wisdom that is within you by the power of the Holy Spirit!!

I love you so much!!!

Love,
Teresa

WOW! The timing of Teresa's note was amazing. It was none other than God speaking through her! In our apartment we had floor-to-ceiling windows with a sweeping view of Lake Michigan. From way up high on the thirty-eighth floor from what we called our "sky cottage," I often stood in that window snapping photo after photo of the gorgeous views. From sunrise to sunset to moon glow over the lake, I always found something beautiful to capture in that lens. Often I would also capture my own reflection while taking the photos. The glare of any lighting, whether from inside or outside, would challenge me to get just the right camera angle to avoid getting myself in the picture. The night before Teresa sent me this email, I was trying to take just the right photo of the waves on the shore of the beach and the glow of the moonlit water. I did manage eventually, but it never ended up being as good as in person. And exactly as Teresa said, the "water . . . gracefully moved about as small waves tossed into each other with such rhythm and peace." Wow!

Yes, that was me she saw in that moonlit window, and she also got to see exactly what I saw! Teresa had no way of knowing any of this! I embraced this word with a grateful heart, thanking God for using Teresa in such a powerful way in my life! I embraced her too—in the spirit, knowing that God had ordained that moment in time for us to see the greatness of our Lord who knows all things!

"Call to me and I will answer you and tell you great and unsearchable things you do not know." (Jeremiah 33:3 NIV)

CHAPTER 11

Chemo #6 — Tomorrow!

From: Lorraine
To: All
Date: November 23, 2015 9:59 PM
Subject: chemo #6 and a short update

Hi family and friends!

Here we go . . . another week flew by! Chemo #6 is tomorrow at 2 p.m. They needed to move me to Tuesday this week because of Thanksgiving and scheduling. Of course, as always, I pray for a smooth, problem-free day and no side effects!

I had a good weekend. The snow came and went. It didn't stick in the city. Those of you who are out in the Chicago suburbs, I know you got at least 15 inches. Hope you were able to get around OK and safely! Thanksgiving is supposed to be in the 50s, so it should be good for travel. To my warm-weather-dwelling family & friends . . . well . . . hope you had another perfect day. ;)

All is well here. I feel good. I got out for some walks this weekend despite the weather. I took another long walk today and just loved it. There is something so invigorating about walking briskly in the winter air.

I hope you all have a wonderful, safe, healthy, and blessed Thanksgiving!

My heart is melted by the love and tenderness you all show toward me and the way you rally around me with so many acts of kindness, encouraging words, notes, faithful prayers, etc.! It's difficult to express it accurately, but my heart bubbles over with joy and gratitude. It's not just now and not just because it's Thanksgiving, but it certainly is a good excuse to say how very thankful I am for you! When God created you, He created a masterpiece. Never forget that! You are unique and special and loved by the One who knitted His tapestry (you) together in such a one-of-a-kind, brilliant, and beautiful way! May you feel His tender touch and may you enjoy reflecting on your blessings as you celebrate this special holiday.

Love,
Lorraine/Rainie

PS: I forgot to mention—based on a few reactions that my veins had to the IVs, the nurses have suggested that I consider a port. Nothing serious, but so far three out of the five veins have had some inflammation afterwards. I asked them why they just don't do a port automatically in everyone, and they said I have excellent veins and should have done well with this IV method. Since I have 13 more treatments, it might be better to protect my veins and do a port. I'm praying for God's wisdom on this decision. It does seem like I'm being led in that direction, but if God doesn't want me to have the port, I believe He will let me know that too. I pray for every single doctor, nurse, anesthesiologist, every member of the medical staff there to be blessed by God with wisdom and excellence. I'm hoping to get another update out before next treatment. It seems there is so much for me to do and to read and to learn about all this as they keep giving me information. So little time, so much to do!

From: Julie A
To: Lorraine
Date: November 24, 2015 7:54 AM
Subject: Re: chemo #6 and a short update

Our God is an awesome God. So I was thrilled but not surprised to read that He has sustained you for another week. One-third of the way through today, Lorraine! What a thing to be thankful for. You have blessed me with your notes, as He came that we might have life and have it more abundantly [from John 10:10] . . . and through your joyous spirit, you reflect that abundance.

We will be thinking of you today and I will be praying this morning as you go your way. I am around so please let me know if you want to walk or need anything at all.

> Because of the Lord's great love we are not consumed, for his compassions never fail. They are new every morning; great is your faithfulness.
> (Lamentations 3:22-23 NIV)

Julie

"... I have come that they may have life, and that they may have it more abundantly."

JOHN 10:10 NKJV

From: Jaime
To: Lorraine
Date: November 24, 2015 8:12 AM
Subject: Re: chemo #6 and a short update

MY SWEET BELLA, I love hearing about your walks. It's one of the things you've always loved doing and one of the most refreshing, mind- and soul-clearing activities we can enjoy. You are ever present on our lips and in our hearts and at the top of our petitions in prayer. I am SO BLESSED with every email from you, every text. Yes, you are "so unique and special and loved by the one who knitted you." I have MUCH to be thankful for regarding His hand in your life. His promises prevail!!!!!!

Xoxo j

From: Natalie
To: Lorraine
Date: November 24, 2015 8:34 AM
Subject: Re: chemo #6 and a short update

I know one thing I'm certainly thankful for this year is that your treatment is not holding you back from enjoying the "little" things in life we can sometimes take for granted and your faith will always keep you strong!! I wish you the best of luck with #6 today and hope you have a wonderful Thanksgiving! Prayers and hugs to you today and always!! Much love from me and my mama. xo

Natalie

From: Kate
To: Lorraine
Date: November 24, 2015 10:18 AM
Subject: Re: chemo #6 and a short update

Hi Lorraine!

Wanted to thank you for the update . . .

You keep moving through this smoothly and with such a gracious heart! I'm praying for you as you make these difficult decisions that are in front of you. And know that you have been making them with God's guidance.

53

I opened my Bible app today, and this is what appeared—a reminder and assurance that victory is ahead:

 . . . but thanks be to God, who gives us the victory through our Lord Jesus Christ.
(1 Corinthians 15:57 NASB)

The true prize and victory awaits. Breathe it in. Sending prayers of strength, courage, and assurance today! As well as many hugs!!

You are an inspiration . . . and I will always thank you for that and for being an example of faith & grace.

xo's,
-Kate :-)

CHAPTER 12

Covered and Surrounded by Grace

Covered

Just before treatments started, I had a to-do list based on what I was learning from my friends Carol, Gail, and Denise, and my cousin Beth—all cancer-conquerors. They suggested that I have my dental exam and cleaning before starting chemo. They also had helpful tips regarding diet, such as eating organic, loading up on veggies and fruits, and staying hydrated with plenty of water, as well as lifestyle habits such as getting exercise when possible and staying positive. I was well equipped with information and most grateful to receive such great tips from my experienced friends and family—words from the wise!

The day of my dental appointment, I also met my friend Pam, who had invited me to go wig shopping at a great little store near her home. At this point everything was still so new to me. It was hard to think that I would have to be wearing a wig soon. Pam wanted to help take a little of the sting out of all that was about to take place. She and her daughters turned the afternoon into one of fun and laughter as I tried on every style and color imaginable. I still had not found the right one, but just as I was about to give up, I noticed a long, straight, medium-blonde "halo" with ombre ends. A halo is a type of headband that fits around the diameter of the head with the hair attached to the band. It is worn with hats. This particular halo was paired with a soft, powder-blue tam. Just for fun I tried it on, and instantly Pam said, "Oh that looks gorgeous on you! You look so young!" That was all I needed to hear! Jokingly I said, "Well then, I'll take it."

Yet, still wanting to find a full wig, I put the halo aside and continued my search. I found two hats I just had to have, so I placed them on the counter and told the sales manager that I was still looking. At that point Pam said, "Girlfriend, you're taking that halo and hat home with you today!"

I replied, "Well, maybe, but I still need to see what else is here."

The manager said, "You *are* taking the hat and halo home with you. She already bought it for you!"

My jaw dropped, and my eyes almost popped out when I said, "What?! How?! When?!"

Pam and the manager, with smiles larger than life, both said, "Yes, it's yours!"

I was dumbfounded that Pam had been able to sneak that by me ("007" is one of my nicknames). With tear-filled eyes I hugged and thanked Pam for this special gift—not only the halo and hat but also the entire afternoon, which was made possible by the generous spirit and love of my precious friend. We both giggled like children as she gave me another bear hug!

So many days with Pam have been fun-filled! My joyful friend and "partner in crime" through the years as we grew up pretending to be Charlie's Angels (she was Jill; I was Kelly). We still are kids at heart!

The halo became my favorite head covering during treatment. It was more comfortable than my full wigs, and I've always been a hat person. I would think of Pam every time I put it on and would smile as my heart danced.

Blanketed

Just before Thanksgiving, with my treatment fully underway, our friends Liz and Brad had a dinner party for a group of us. This group began many years ago with just a few single women coming together to learn, share, and experience life through Bible study and fellowship. The group became rock solid, and the relationships flourished. We remain close to this day as we walk through life together and support each other in tangible as well as spiritual ways. Through the years we each got married, doubling the size of our group. Our personal journeys have taken us in different directions . . . but never separated us from the bond of friendship that was birthed so long ago.

The pre-Thanksgiving dinner party was a great way to enjoy one another's company, to celebrate all of the blessings we've been given, and to recognize our gift of friendship. I couldn't have imagined how deeply blessed I would be on that evening. They all lifted me up in a special prayer for my healing. Liz—always thinking of others, and now especially my needs—made sure the dinner was a complete, healthy feast. After dinner the girls presented me with cards filled with encouragement and a cozy, plush, snow-white blanket to wrap myself in through the winter months and through treatment as I rested in the God of all comfort. I call it my "blanket of grace!" I still use this blanket, and each time I snuggle up inside of it, I feel God's warmth embracing me and His grace covering me.

I thank God for these loving women as I mention them by name every day. I ask Him to let them know how much He loves each of them and let them feel the same soft embrace of His grace—always!

Let us be concerned for one another, to help one another to show love and to do good. (Hebrews 10:24 GNT)

Anointed

One warm afternoon in early December—which felt like May with a temperature of 60—my friend Denise drove into the city to see me. We had a lovely lunch at a nearby café. When we returned to my apartment, she presented me with a huge gift basket, filled with an array of gifts for all of the senses—a basket full of love. She also had a strong desire to pray for me and asked me if she could anoint me with oil. Although I had already received that anointing and prayer from the elders of my church, I gladly accepted her offer. Her beautiful prayer for my healing was shorter than she had planned. When she finished, she said that during the prayer, she felt the Spirit of God tell her, "It is already done." As she spoke those words, my eyes filled with tears, and with a wide smile I said, "I have accepted it!" We hugged and thanked God for His love and mercy and for all that He has provided!

Let us be concerned for one another, to help one another to show love and to do good.

HEBREWS 10:24 GNT

I thanked God for Denise also, and I continue to thank Him for blessing my life with such a beautiful, faithful friend and sister! How lovely she is and how sweet our friendship remains.

Encircled

As treatment proceeded, I was made aware of how many people were praying for me. So many friends and family members were also asking their friends to pray for my healing. I was amazed! I felt privileged to see what God was exposing to me: a depth of character, grace, love, and faith flowing from these compassionate hearts praying for *me*! How do you thank them? How can you accurately express what your heart really feels? I found myself thanking them over and over again. I felt the love (God-given and pure) for these faithful souls rising inside of me and spilling over! Only God can do this!

As I mentioned to my "group" of prayer warriors how I was feeling as I was finding out about these growing prayer chains, they said, "Yes, girlfriend, we've got you covered." It was during this conversation that I learned about their continuous circle of prayer for me. They told me that they'd been praying for me nonstop during their waking hours since I'd told them about the cancer. They chose their personal prayer times and set their alarms on their phones with a note: *"Pray for Lorraine."* As soon as one person would finish, the next would start. Some would even text the next in line to say, *"I'm handing it over to you now."* WOW! Again, there is no adequate way to describe my gratitude!

Here is a portion of the thread they shared when beginning their daily prayer chain:

On Oct 8, 2015, at 8:26 AM, Liz wrote:

I like the different suggestions below.

Can we agree to commit ourselves to praying specifically for Lorraine and her needs (based on her updates she sends us) on the hour every 4 hours??

Melissa laid it out well. If we start at 6:00 am (I am fine with the early shift because I am up and leaving the gym around that time), we could each take every 4th hour up to 9:00 pm every day in prayer for her.

If we go with this plan, how about we lay it out like this:

> *Liz 6 am, 10 am, 2 pm, 6 pm*
> *Pam 7 am, 11 am, 3 pm, 7 pm*
> *Mariellen 8 am, 12 pm, 4 pm, 8 pm*
> *Melissa 9 am, 1 pm, 5 pm, 9 pm*

I am thinking these times based on when we get up to go to work or take care of the kids, etc. Please let me know if this works for each of you and we will begin the prayer warrior chain for Lorraine!!

After they unanimously agreed to this schedule, Liz sent out the following confirmation:

So we have our watches synchronized for our times . . . Let the praying begin, my faithful prayer warrior Besties!!! Love, Liz

Surrounded

There were other prayer chains also—from friends in Bible study groups who faithfully prayed for me and even called me to pray over the phone. There were people I didn't even know, who had found out about the concern of a loved one over me, and compassionately responded in prayer and in spreading the word to others to pray!

How can I possibly find the room in this book to mention every single person by name? How can I explain the creative ways people loved us through this time? Every single person in my life played an important role in this story! My heart is full of gratitude!

CHAPTER 13

Chemo #6 — A Good Day!

From: Lorraine
To: All
Date: November 25, 2015 11:54 AM
Subject: Chemo #6 . . . a good day!

Yay . . . a good day . . .

Chemo six was A-OK! ☺

It went quickly and smoothly with NO problems. Multiple prayers were answered throughout the day and I felt blessed as God's hand was upon me. I felt the working of the many faithful prayers being spoken on my behalf. God is working!!!!

I will be getting a port put in right after Thanksgiving. I'll let you know when that will be when they call to confirm me regarding scheduling. I have 12 more to go. For that reason the general consensus among the chemo nurses is that I need to preserve my veins and a port will be the best way to do that.

My next LONG treatment day will be next Wednesday, December 2nd. I'll start at 8:00 a.m. for labs, then the doctor's exam, then the long treatment. This one is always a bit tougher for me (not a morning person ;)). Otherwise I pray and expect it to go well.

The weeks are flying by. I'm now one-third of the way through! Yay!

I pray now for another good reading on my cancer blood marker, since it came down significantly last time we checked it. They do say it is just a trend . . . like watching the stock market. But I still want to see it come down, down, down!!!

Thank you all once again! Greg and I both send you our love and will be mentioning all of you in our long list of gratitudes! We mention you all by name, and we thank God for even those we do not know who are praying for us in your many prayer chains (amazing)!!!

Have a wonderful Thanksgiving!

Love,
Lorraine/Rainie (and Greg too)

From: David
To: Lorraine
Date: November 29, 2015 1:17 PM
Subject: Re: Chemo #6 . . . a good day!

Lorraine,

You are a real trooper! I applaud your resolve and sense of "attack and conquer." That is the best way to go about such an event!

I know where your strength comes from and I pray that God continues to provide it as well as a positive ultimate result!

Blessings,
David

From: Kathy S
To: Lorraine
Date: December 1, 2015 5:43 AM
Subject: Re: Chemo #6 . . . a good day!

Praying with you as I read your words, in Jesus's name, "holding your hands" up to our Father, His Son, & the Holy Spirit. Amen.

CHAPTER 14

Chemo #7 — A Great Day!

From: Lorraine
To: All
Date: December 2, 2015 8:10 PM
Subject: Chemo #7 . . . A Great Day!

Hi everyone!

Today was wonderfully blessed! It went quickly and effortlessly, no reactions of any kind. I had my favorite IV nurse who inserted my IV with no issues. During my oncologist visit he said I'm doing great and everything checked out very good. My blood work was very good, and you may remember that before I started chemo, my CA125 (blood test for cancer marker) was 535; then after the 1st cycle (3 weeks) it dropped more than half to 236. Today . . . DRUM ROLL PLEASE . . . it dropped again all the way down to 48!

I was so happy, I cried tears of joy! What a huge blessing I received today! A day full of blessings—huge blessings, small blessings, and every other size in between! They are all blessings to be grateful for . . . and I am . . . I am!!!

When we left today, as we walked home the skies cleared and the sun came out, shining brightly above us as if a smile from God as He illuminated our path! JOY, JOY, JOY!!!

Your prayers are giving me strength. You are encouraging me in such beautiful ways. Your faith is shining brightly just as the sun did today! Thank you for covering me with a blanket of warm, comforting grace as you give away the love in your hearts! May God illuminate your paths.

> "The Lord bless you and keep you; the Lord make his face shine on you and be gracious to you; the Lord turn his face toward you and give you peace."
> (Numbers 6:24-26 NIV)

Love,
Lorraine/Rainie

From: Dr. Kehoe
To: Lorraine
Date: December 2, 2015 9:02 PM
Subject: Re: Chemo #7 . . . A Great Day!

You continue to inspire!! I love the CA125 drop and that you are tolerating the chemotherapy so well and with such good cheer. You prove the power of prayer.

Bill

PS: Did you get the port?

From: Pastor Lutzer
To: Lorraine
Date: December 3, 2015 9:49 AM
Subject: Message from Pastor

Lorraine, I pray that this Christmas season would be one in which your heart continues to be uplifted by God's grace and power. I also pray that these treatments would work so well that you might be able to look back on this as a real gift of God giving you the gift of life.

I pray that you and Greg have a blessed Christmas!

Pastor

From: Kathy S
To: Lorraine
Date: December 3, 2015 6:02 AM
Subject: Re: Chemo #7 . . . A Great Day!

Lorraine, thinking of you & thanking our Father for His extraordinary individual love for you, His precious daughter, Lorraine Brown / Rainie . . . "for your Father knows what you need before you ask him" [Matthew 6:8 NIV]. Praying for His guidance & provision throughout each day, in Jesus's name.

I love you,
Kathy xo

"... for your Father knows what you need before you ask him."

MATTHEW 6:8 NIV

From: Aunt Betty and Uncle Orville
To: Lorraine
Date: December 2, 2015 10:28 PM
Subject: Re: Chemo #7 . . . A Great Day!

Our Dear Rainie,

Tears of JOY here! What a joyful day for all of us. This is what we pray for! Thank You, God. You do hear our pleas and Your strong answers ring true. Thank You, thank You, thank You! Today we have joy and peace—the peace that passes all understanding.

Much Love
Betty and Orville

From: Susie
To: Lorraine
Date: December 2, 2015 9:53 PM
Subject: Re: Chemo #7 . . . A Great Day!

Oh Rainie! I'm so happy to read your news, I'm crying right along with you!!! Remarkable how your numbers have dropped! You are almost within the normal range and I say Hallelujah!!! Praise God!! I couldn't be happier for you and will keep sending the prayers your way, sweet cousin! You are healing so quickly and He is the reason! I'm a believer in the power of prayer and so many people are rallying around you in prayer and it's working!

I love you!!! You're are an amazingly beautiful inspiration!!

Ahh . . . sweet dreams to you & Greg!

Sus

From: Harry
To: Lorraine
Date: December 3, 2015 6:24 AM
Subject: Re: Chemo #7 . . . A Great Day!

I just LOVE to get an email with "A Great Day" written in the subject box! Lorraine, I am so encouraged for you by this praise report! God is sooooo faithful (but we already knew that ☺)!

I understand some of the original words of caution regarding the "blood count marker," but these numbers seem far too dramatic to be misunderstood. On a side note I sure wish my cholesterol count would come down this dramatically! (Can u pray for me now? LOL)

I know there's a temptation for us to pull back a little on prayers when things start to look positive, but we are all aware that this is a battle on 2 levels—physical and spiritual . . . and it never lets up . . . so our prayers grow stronger!!

God's blessings on you today and through your remaining treatments!

Praising God!
Harry

From: Jaime
To: Lorraine
Date: December 3, 2015 8:40 AM
Subject: Re: Chemo #7 . . . A Great Day!

JOY JOY JOY!!!! I can't get enough of these good reports, GOD IS SO GOOD, SO FAITHFUL, SO LOVING, SO MERCIFUL!!!! I thank Him every day for your healing. I pray for an extra measure of strength and courage to walk the path set before you, I pray for your rays of light to shine brighter than ever, and they do!!! You are so loved, sister!!!

From: Natalie
To: Lorraine
Date: December 3, 2015, 8:48 AM
Subject: Re: Chemo #7 . . . A Great Day!

WOW—that is wonderful news!!!

I got chills reading those numbers (after the drum roll). ;) I pray the remaining treatment days stay "uneventful" and smooth—I KNOW they will! God bless, and keep the updates coming! My mom looks forward to them each week . . . and always prays they stay as positive and wonderful as you are!! Love and hugs—mwah!!!

Natalie

From: Judy B
To: Lorraine
Date: December 3, 2015 9:35 AM
Subject: Woohoo!!

Thanks for sharing the good news, Lorraine! I am rejoicing with you. You have been on my mind the last few days and I have turned those thoughts into prayers for you. Your Father certainly is looking down on you and smiling. May He continue to bless and touch you with His healing hand until the marker is down to 0!! I am so glad you haven't had any strong reactions to the treatments. I know God is using your joy and trust in Him to point others to Himself. To God be the glory—great things He has done!

With love and prayers, Judy

From: Kathy B
To: Lorraine
Date: December 3, 2015 9:53 AM
Subject: Re: Chemo #7 . . . A Great Day!

48!!! I will take that number and do cartwheels around it.

You mentioned your favorite IV nurse, which means no port yet??? Can you request her every time?

Love,
Kathy

From: Julie W
To: Lorraine
Date: December 3, 2015 10:39 AM
Subject: Yesterday

Hi Lorraine, what a blessing it was to me to be with you yesterday! It's been so long since we have seen each other and it was so great to see you and catch up. It's like we never left off, and great friends are like that and stay together and connected no matter what. I love you so much and am so proud of how you are handling all this. However, even if you have some bad days where you are down, that is OK—and give yourself permission and acceptance and forgiveness if and when that should happen. The Lord will also understand. But your true inner nature as a woman of God is evident to me and to others around you. What a testimony!

Wow, what a blessing that your cancer marker went down so much! Praise God! And the treatment went so smooth yesterday. The time just flew by and it was very pleasant to be there and to have lunch together. You are amazing and I love you and let me know if I can help you in any way in the future!!!!

Hugs and prayers!
Julie

From: Pam (Angel/Jill) ;)
To: Lorraine (Angel/Kelly) ;)
Date: December 3, 2015 7:18 PM
Subject: Re: Chemo #7 . . . A Great Day!

oh . . . this is the BEST news for me!!! what a beautiful answer to prayer!!:) just WOW,

Angel!!!!! wow!!! the #'s are amazing!!!!

i will call ya later or tomorrow! miss you and want to see you! must find a way to come visit or something!!! K?

just so glad to see how all your care/good works and God's amazing movement are working for you! you always take such stellar good care of yourself—i learn from yououououou!!! i'm sure it all is coming together in this wonderful answer to prayer! oxoxxooxoxoxoxoxoxox

Jill

CHAPTER 15

The Port

From: Lorraine
To: All
Date: December 4, 2015 8:31 AM
Subject: The Port

Many of you have asked about the port. It probably doesn't seem as though it should be a difficult decision for me to make regarding going forward with it, especially after having inflammation with some of my veins. I did tell the nurses that I would go ahead with it. I called scheduling last Friday but they didn't call me back until Monday. They were not able put me on the schedule for another week—the following Monday.

I've been praying for clarity on this because I really don't like the idea of a surgical procedure, especially now that treatments are well underway. At this point there is some risk involved.

During my oncology exam this week, my doctor said I'm doing great and he also said, "You have excellent veins. I'm not sure why you are doing a port." I explained that the nurses seem to think it will be easier for me going forward. He replied, "Well, it's your decision." I told him I sure wish he would make that decision for me (then I thought, *Well, if he could make the decision for me, he would probably not do it. . . . Hmmmm.*).

When I got to treatment, my IV went in perfectly. The last three visits have gone so smoothly that I began to rethink this port issue. I've prayed that God would give me peace about doing the port, but that if it is not for me, He would give me the confidence to go forward without it.

I realized that I am the only one with the authority to make this decision, and I also realized that God would protect me either way. The words that my oncologist spoke resonated with me. I kept hearing those words, "You have excellent veins. I'm not sure why you are doing a port." Hearing that from my doctor, and then replaying it in my mind, gave me the peace to call and cancel the port procedure. I trust that I made the right decision.

When I entered the chemo room over the past three great visits, I felt God telling me to let go! I prayed, "Yes, God, You are my IV nurse, my physician, my healer. Here is my arm. You insert the IV and I'll receive the medicine. I know ALL is well with You, Lord."

I had to surrender! I had to stop fearing that needle! I even said (and out loud), "Fear is NOT allowed in heaven; therefore it is NOT allowed in me!!!"

Amazing what surrendering will do!

Thank you all for your prayers of support in this decision. I know you were asking the Lord to allow me to hear His wisdom clearly on this issue!

I walk forward now, telling my veins to obey! ☺

I love you all!
Lorraine/Rainie

CHAPTER 16

Chemo #8 Is Today!

From: Lorraine
To: All
Date: December 9, 2015 10:58 AM
Subject: Chemo 8 is today

Hi family and friends!

I was thinking about last week and I should have titled chemo #7 "a gift from heaven" because with my cancer marker (CA125) coming all the way down to 48, this was and is truly a gift! I received that gift with great joy! An early Christmas gift!

Today at 2:00 p.m. is my next session . . . chemo #8. Let it be great!

I hope you are all enjoying this "gift" of a gorgeous day! Especially here in Chicago . . . we're having temps in the 50s with clear skies and bright sunshine! Wow! Yet . . . every day is a gift!

Thank you all for your constant prayers and love!

This is the day which the Lord hath made; we will rejoice and be glad in it.
(Psalm 118:24 KJV)

Love,
Lorraine/Rainie

From: Laura D
To: Lorraine
Date: December 9, 2015 11:19 AM
Subject: Re: Chemo 8 is today

I love you, my friend, and already have you prayed up for this afternoon!

From: Jaime
To: Lorraine
Date: December 9, 2015 12:28 PM
Subject: Re: Chemo 8 is today

What a gift He continues to give, HE IS FAITHFUL!!! PRAYING YOU THROUGH MY SWEET SISTER. LOVE YOU!!!!!! You're in my thoughts every day, every single day!!!!

xoxoxoxo j

From: Linda
To: Lorraine
Date: December 9, 2015 1:12 PM
Subject: Re: Chemo 8 is today

Lorraine,

It was a gift for all of us to hear that wonderful news! Could not ask for anything better this Christmas! Love you and you are in our hearts and prayers always but especially during your treatment in a little bit.

With much love,
Linda ♡ ♡ ♡

From: Tom
To: Lorraine
Date: December 9, 2015 1:57 PM
Subject: Re: Chemo 8 is today

Way to go Lorraine. God's doing His deal.

Blessings
Tom

From: Bruce R
To: Lorraine
Date: December 9, 2015 6:53 PM
Subject: Re: Chemo 8 is today

Yes, we shall rejoice in this and all days! Hang tough, Kiddo! We're all pulling and praying for you!

CHAPTER 17

Chemo #8 Was Great!

From: Lorraine
To: All
Date: December 10, 2015 8:47 PM
Subject: Update . . . chemo 8 was great!

Hi everyone!

Chemo 8 was great! No issues of any kind! Praise God!

Next Wednesday, we will be celebrating the halfway point and we will also be celebrating Greg's birthday. It will be a unique birthday for him, but since it's a weekday, he says it's just fine. He did request a Pizano's Pizza, so I'll be happy to accommodate. It will be low key but we will make up for it soon and there will be a great deal of celebrating to do!

I hope you all enjoyed another beautiful day. Spring-like weather again today here! Love it!

Thank you all for praying me/us through another week! You are all in our constant prayers as well.

Love and Hugs to all of you!
Lorraine/Rainie

From: Sandy O
To: Lorraine
Date: December 11, 2015, 6:58 AM
Subject: Re: Update . . . chemo 8 was great!

Such good news, Lorraine! Look at you . . . already to the halfway point next week!!! You're doing a great job!!!

God is soooo good!

Love you!
Sandy

From: Natalie
To: Lorraine
Date: December 11, 2015, 10:55 AM
Subject: Re: Update . . . chemo 8 was great!

Woo hoo! Loving these updates—and I know more wonderful news is on the way each week! Love you and have a fabulous weekend. ;) mwah!

From: Mariellen
To: Lorraine
Date: December 14, 2015, 9:09 PM
Subject: Re: Update . . . chemo 8 was great!

Hi Lorraine,

Just praying for you tonight and looking forward to hearing good news of how God will be caring for you this week in your treatment.

How are you feeling? I am looking forward to seeing you again in the new year. Hoping you and Greg have a wonderful Christmas and looking forward to seeing how God will bless you in the new year!

Praying Jeremiah 30:17 (ESV) for you tonight my dear friend: "For I will restore health to you, and your wounds I will heal, declares the Lord."

Love you,
Mariellen

From: Kathy S
To: Lorraine
Date: December 16, 2015, 5:46 AM
Subject: Re: Update . . . chemo 8 was great!

Sweet Lorraine~

Praying that #9 will be fine.

Romans 15:13 (ESV): "May the God of hope fill you with all joy and peace in believing, so that by the power of the Holy Spirit you may abound in hope."

So thankful for all the details our God has covered up to this time. He goes before you.

With love, my dear friend,
Kathy ♡

CHAPTER 18

Chemo #9 Was Mighty Fine!

From: Lorraine
To: All
Date: December 19, 2015 2:01 PM
Subject: update: chemo nine was mighty fine

Hi family and friends!

Just a quick note to let you know that Wednesday's treatment went fine. I woke that morning to clouds and light rain, but as the afternoon approached, the weather cleared. The sun came out and smiled on Greg on his birthday. He arrived just in time for my treatment. I had a very kind nurse and it went quickly and smoothly. Praise God! I surprised Greg with his favorite Portillo's chocolate cake, which was waiting for him when we got home. Simple pleasures. He's still smiling. Some of you are all too familiar with his "chocolate cake smile." ;)

My next treatment is Wednesday the 23rd. It will be the long, 2-drug day. I have to be there bright and early. Praying, as always, for a smooth, successful day.

Keeping you all in prayer . . . that you remain healthy, for safe travel, and you see the blessings all around you in every moment!

Love you all!
Lorraine/Rainie

From: Dr. Kehoe
To: Lorraine
Date: December 19, 2015 2:28 PM
Subject: Re: update: chemo nine was mighty fine

You continue to amaze and inspire.

Bill

From: Mary
To: Lorraine
Date: December 19, 2015 2:42 PM
Subject: Re: update: chemo nine was mighty fine

Praise the Lord. Praying for a Christmas miracle!

From: Phyllis
To: Lorraine
Date: December 19, 2015 4:33 PM
Subject: Re: update: chemo nine was mighty fine

Prayer-hearing, prayer-answering, miracle-working GOD. Thank You, Lord, for Lorraine's treatment, caring nurse, and the "smooth, successful day." Love hearing the good news. Will keep you always in my prayers and keep praying for me too.

hugs, hugs, hugs,
Phyllis

From: Kathy S
To: Lorraine
Date: December 19, 2015 9:03 PM
Subject: Re: chemo nine was mighty fine

Thank you so much for the update, Lorraine! So glad to hear #9 was fine. As for Greg I am very familiar with the Portillo's chocolate cake smile . . . for I have experienced that myself! ☺ So glad you could celebrate together. You 2 are so beautiful together! ♡ we love you both! xo

---

From: Becky
To: Lorraine
Date: December 20, 2015 7:32 AM
Subject: Re: update: chemo nine was mighty fine

Praise God, Lorraine! Good luck with the treatment on the 23rd. I will be praying for you as always.

Becky

From: Jaime
To: Lorraine
Date: December 20, 2015 12:52 PM
Subject: Re: update: chemo nine was mighty fine

I am so overjoyed! Happy birthday, Greg!!!! Praying abundant blessings!!! Thanking Jesus and rejoicing chemo nine went well. The prayers continue DAILY!!! Love you so much!!!!

From: Aunt Betty and Uncle Orville
To: Lorraine
Date: December 20, 2015 4:56 PM
Subject: Re: update: chemo nine was mighty fine

Hi!

Truly you are blessed, Rainie! We who love you believe that our prayers have been granted by a loving and merciful God.

Love,
Aunt Betty and Uncle Orville—hoping to see you on Christmas

From: Harry
To: Lorraine
Date: December 22, 2015 10:31 AM
Subject: Re: update: chemo nine was mighty fine

Hi Lorraine! Again, we are all so happy that the treatment went well last week. I'm really loving the "consistency"!!!! I know you mentioned that the treatment tomorrow will be a long one . . . so we'll pray even harder!

Yes . . . I do remember Greg's chocolate cake smile. In fact I have a picture to prove it! I was looking for it to send to you, but couldn't seem to find it. One of these days I'll send it when you least expect it! Ha-ha!

Lorraine . . . I am looking forward to seeing you both soon. Let's try to be creative in making that happen! LOL!

Have a special and memorable Christmas as you celebrate our Savior's birth!

In Him, Harry

CHAPTER 19

Chemo #10 — We'll Try Again

From: Lorraine
To: All
Date: December 23, 2015 10:32 PM
Subject: Update and Christmas blessing!

MERRY CHRISTMAS FRIENDS AND FAMILY! I hope your hearts are filled with joy and peace and your homes are filled with love and laughter! May you enjoy the celebration of the best gift ever given!

Quick update: chemo ten . . . we'll try again . . .

I wasn't able to have chemo on Wednesday because my white blood count was low. The doctor said to come back next week and we will resume, providing my counts are normal. Praying that they will be and that we do not have to delay treatment again. It was strange to hear those words. I was really bummed. My oncologist said, "It's interesting . . . when people first hear the words they need chemo, they don't want it, but during treatment if they are told they need to miss a week, they are so disappointed." LOL! So true. Well, I told him we just don't want to delay progress.

It was an odd morning. I was very tired because I had to be there at 7:40 for labs, then a doctor visit to be followed by treatment. I didn't sleep well the night before, anticipating having to get up and hoping the alarm(s) went off. No matter how early I go to bed, I struggle with early calls—I've never been an early-morning person.

But I do have some GOOD NEWS . . . Despite the crazy morning God showed everyone who's boss . . . because . . . I received an email with my test results from my blood cancer marker (CA125) and it came all the way down to 15.7. HALLELUJAH!!!!!! The normal range is 0–30, so I'm in the normal range!!! Praise God!!! Friends and Family, I'm NORMAL! ;)

When I opened that email with the test result, I dropped to my knees and cried tears of JOY, praising God for THIS BLESSED CHRISTMAS GIFT and answer to prayer!

Thinking of each of you and keeping you in my prayers for a wonderfully blessed Christmas!

Love,
Lorraine (Rainie)

 "For unto you is born this day in the city of David a Savior, who is Christ the Lord."
(Luke 2:11 ESV)

PS: We will miss our families, as we will be staying home on both Christmas Eve and Christmas Day based on my white counts. Greg was able to make a quick trip out during the day to deliver presents and have a quick visit with Aunt Betty and Uncle Orville. I'm so glad he did that.

From: Aunt Betty and Uncle Orville
To: Lorraine
Date: December 26, 2015 9:45 PM
Subject: Re: Update and Christmas blessing!

Dear ones,

Have you noticed that Christmas comes whether you are ready or not? We couldn't wait till one more batch of cookies got baked, or a package got wrapped, or the one who was sick felt well. It came with shouts of greetings, hugs, and lots of noise—not a silent night! But oh how joyful a time of togetherness, never troubling about a missing cookie but sincerely caring about those we love who could not be with us this year. Saying a prayer for healing, every head bowed.

We are most grateful for getting to visit with Greg. Haven't missed a Christmas together since he was a toddler.

Uncle Orville and I are very touched by the lovely gifts from you two. We marvel that you found time to provide gifts for all of us. The glass bowl is quite unique and we will see if we can fill it with the assorted nuts or M&Ms. Thank you, thank you!

May 2016 be a happy new year with healing and a joyous wedding for Laura and Kyle in August.

Lots of Love
Aunt Betty

From: Becky
To: Lorraine
Date: December 25, 2015 9:58 PM
Subject: Re: Update and Christmas blessing!

Lorraine, maybe God knew you didn't need that tenth treatment just then? Merry Christmas to you and your family. God bless you. I will keep saying prayers for all of you. Take care of yourself.

Love, Becky

From: Kathy B
To: Lorraine
Date: December 26, 2015 8:50 AM
Subject: Re: Update and Christmas blessing!

I need to ask at what point in your life did you become normal? As when we were kids growing up together, neither of us were very normal. ;)

From: Jaime
To: Lorraine
Date: December 26, 2015 8:53 AM
Subject: Re: Update and Christmas blessing!

Tears of JOY alongside you my sweet sister!!!! Thank you for these updates. They mean so very much! I am sending all my love and Merry Christmas wishes, and prayers for a very HAPPY, HEALTHY and BLESSED NEW YEAR!

xoxo j

From: Maenon
To: Lorraine
Date: December 26, 2015 11:36 AM
Subject: Christmas wonder . . .

Dear Rainie, what a wonderful Christmas gift. And no one deserves it more than you. Your beliefs and faith in God are testaments of such great belief. It is truly a present sent to you. My very best wishes for the coming year and hope that you and Greg have peace and contentment always . . .

With great love, Maenon

From: Debby
To: Lorraine
Date: December 26, 2015 3:21 PM
Subject: Re: Update and Christmas blessing!

Merry Christmas, Lorraine! I'm so uplifted to hear of your good news. Even with the disappointment with the delayed treatment, overall there's no better present from Jesus than the miracle of your healing. Glory!

Love you!!!!!!!

From: Lisa
To: Lorraine
Date: December 27, 2015 3:21 PM
Subject: Re: Update and Christmas blessing!

What a wonderful Christmas gift . . . you are NORMAL ☺!!!!!

I am praying for continued progress for you. This is such beautiful news! Merry Christmas to you and Greg.

Love you

From: Nancy
To: Lorraine
Date: December 27, 2015 7:35 PM
Subject: Re: Update and Christmas blessing!

Hi Lorraine,

Great news!!! Love to hear your joy! I hope you had a great Christmas and let me know how this week goes! Happy new year and praying for a very blessed 2016!

Nancy

From: Natalie
To: Lorraine
Date: December 28, 2015 9:56 AM
Subject: Re: Update and Christmas blessing!

NORMAL RANGE—That is one of the best presents this year!!!!! I know the delay in treatment was a bummer but you'll be rested and ready to take it on this week. Prayers and hugs to you and Greg!!

XOXOXO!! Nat

82

From: Ruth
To: Lorraine
Date: December 31, 2015 9:40 AM
Subject: Re: Update and Christmas blessing!

Merry Christmas to you a few days late!

I was praying and thinking of you yesterday and hope that your count was good, so as not to delay treatment. You are on my mind and heart every day, and each time I think of you I breathe a prayer for strength and healing. I hope you were able to have a restful Christmas.

A very Happy New Year to you both! Maybe we can speak by phone sometime this weekend. My love and prayers to you both!

Love, Ruth E.

From: Phyllis
To: Lorraine
Date: December 31, 2015 9:50 AM
Subject: Re: Update and Christmas blessing!

> "For I know the plans I have for you," declares the Lord, "plans to prosper you and not to harm you, plans to give you hope and a future."
> (Jeremiah 29:11 NIV)

Seek the Lord, pray to Him, and trust in His good plans for you . . . He still needs you here on the earth. Praying for normal white blood counts . . .

What a "marathon" you're running. You go, girl! You're doing great.

Love you,
Phyllis

CHAPTER 20

Chemo #10 Got an 11

From: Lorraine
To: All
Date: December 31, 2015 12:13 PM
Subject: chemo 10 got an 11

Hi everyone . . .

A quick update regarding chemo 10. Although I had to miss last week's session due to the low white count, it was a nice break and such a timely blessing to not have it right before Christmas.

We were able to resume treatment yesterday. All my blood counts came back in the normal range. Chemo 10 was completed and it all went smoothly.

Interestingly, the lab did another CA125 (blood test cancer marker) because I had a different tech who was not aware that it was done last week. I get it checked once every three weeks at the beginning of each cycle. Understandably this lab tech didn't know they did this test last week. Well . . . it came in at 11.5. As you may recall, it was 15.7 last week. It came down more, even with a week off of chemo! Amazing! Thank You, Lord!!!

My friend Liz said, "Not only did you get a wonderful Christmas gift but now a New Year's gift as well!" So true! I'm completely humbled by His grace and mercy!

May each and every one of you receive the abundant Joy of the Lord as you enter into a new year and may His light shine in you and through you every day!

Happy New Year with deepest appreciation and Love to you all!
Lorraine (Rainie)

From: Aunt Betty and Uncle Orville
To: Lorraine
Date: December 31, 2015 9:12 PM
Subject: Re: chemo 10 got an 11

Dear Rainie,

There have been big signs saying "BELIEVE" placed about in advertising, and now with your news, Rainie, it may influence more folks.

We are so thankful for answered prayers and the gifts of courage and faith that you display every day. God bless us every one!

Love and continued prayers for healing,
Aunt Betty

From: Kate
To: Lorraine
Date: December 31, 2015 7:28 PM
Subject: Re: chemo 10 got an 11

Hi Lorraine!

This is such great news!!

Amazing Christmas gift and a wonderful start to 2016 . . . God's healing hand is on you! YOU are courageous, faithful, strong, and always full of love . . . true inspiration!

Happy New Year!!

Much love to you and Greg . . .
xo, —Kate :-)

From: Dr. Kehoe
To: Lorraine
Date: December 31, 2015 2:55 PM
Subject: Re: chemo 10 got an 11

Lorraine,

The good news just keeps on coming!!! Happy healthy new year to you, Greg, and your family.

Bill

From: Debby
To: Lorraine
Date: December 31, 2015 12:25 PM
Subject: Re: chemo 10 got an 11

Whoa, such good news! I'm so happy for you. I guess God doesn't need chemo in order to heal someone. He's pushing on ahead without it. Praying for a blessed and happy new year for you. Love you.

From: Charlotte
To: Lorraine
Date: December 31, 2015 12:30 PM
Subject: Re: chemo 10 got an 11

Lorraine,

You are always in my prayers. I wish for you this new year an excellent recovery and a renewal of creative spirit.

You deserve the best!

Fondly,
Charlotte

From: Kathy S
To: Lorraine
Date: December 31, 2015 11:31 PM
Subject: Re: chemo 10 got an 11

Yaaaaaay!!! Thank You, Lord Jesus, for great news!!! So thankful, Lorraine!

Sleep in heavenly peace

From: Sandy O
To: Lorraine
Date: January 1, 2016 6:50 AM
Subject: Re: chemo 10 got an 11

That is great news, Lorraine! Lots of answered prayers right there! What time did you get done? Did you have your favorite RN? Now to celebrate all that God has done in 2015 and to put 2016 into His loving hands!

Love you!

From: Lorraine
To: Sandy O
Date: January 1, 2016 11:01 AM
Subject: Re: Re: chemo 10 got an 11

Hi Sandy,

Amen! Many answered prayers. In fact, yes, I did get my favorite RN! My private prayer was that she would be my nurse this week, and praise God, I started with her as my IV nurse, and then Kathryn (I did not have her before) administered the chemo and she was wonderful too.

I pray differently over each session now as I trust God to be my RN and my IV inserter as the Holy Spirit reminds me that God is my physician and He is everything! I know He will lead me to the right place at the right time with the right people. This includes the right nurse for me on that day. Remember back when I told you that I had to surrender this to God? The Holy Spirit reminded me not to get tricked by any trace of fear as I enter into each treatment session, and as I claim to pray in faith, I must stay in faith. God is so gracious and merciful.

Amen . . . let us celebrate all God has done and put 2016 into His loving hands!

Thanks so much, Sandy! I am thanking God for you as I count all my blessings from 2015! I pray for health and Christ's abundant Life for all of you!

I love you!
Lorraine

CHAPTER 21

#11 Complete—Oh How Sweet!

From: Lorraine
To: All
Date: January 7, 2016 4:39 PM
Subject: update: 11 complete, oh how sweet

Hi family and friends!

Chemo 11 complete . . . oh how sweet!

It went great. So many answered prayers. My white blood count was at a good normal number! Praise God. Everything went smoothly and the nurse was great. They assigned me the nurse I actually replaced in a previous session because I was uncomfortable with her. I suppose enough time has gone by that they thought it would be OK to put her back in to the rotation. Well, she was terrific! I have been praying for her and all the nurses there.

Before I head over there, I have to remind myself to surrender. I pray, "God, You are my protector, provider, healer, my ALL! I release this to You! You will choose my nurses and give me the ones You want me to have today." Well, when I got there today and they told me who my nurse would be, I got a lump in my throat. After the nursing aide took my vitals and left the room, I sat there alone and I heard the Holy Spirit say, "Who are you trusting?" I silently replied, "YOU, LORD." I took a deep breath and relaxed in submission. He took care of me. When the nurse came in, the IV went in smoothly and comfortably, and we made small talk and she was very nice and extremely professional. The day proceeded smoothly.

Greg arrived a few minutes later and saw that I was just fine (I had texted him about the situation). We both smiled a knowing smile that God and I had a moment. A moment of testing. A moment of surrender. A moment of resting in the knowledge that there is NOTHING God can't do!

In that place . . . the Holy Spirit had to bring me back to reality and presented me with the question, "Do you have Faith that God can do anything . . . all things?" I replied in silence, "Yes, of course." He continued to speak to my spirit: "If you believe I am able to do anything, then you can trust that I can do it! Fear NOT, for I am with you." I rested in Christ as He worked it all out.

As the day moved along, our conversations were even more relaxed and pleasant. I thanked her for being so kind and for her great care of me.

God blessed us with another sunny day as He carried me there and then walked Greg and me home along the same path we've treaded for 11 weeks now . . . together, arm in arm following HIM, warmed by His light . . . the light of His Spirit in us and the light of the sunshine He created to warm us. It was a sweet day. Glory to God! I hope you are all basking in the warmth of His presence!

Sending hugs and lots of love!
Lorraine

From: Lisa
To: Lorraine
Date: January 8, 2016 10:14 AM
Subject: Re: update: 11 complete, oh how sweet

This is so beautiful, Rainie! Your faith in God is and will be what gets you through this all. We pray for you and think of you always. I love you! Keep that positive spirit and faith going strong. I love your updates; they give me strength. I am so happy to hear that your white cell counts are normal! This is wonderful news.

Love you so much!!!!

From: Jaime
To: Lorraine
Date: January 8, 2016 1:00 PM
Subject: Re: update: 11 complete, oh how sweet

Your emails bring tears to my eyes every time. God's goodness is magnified time and again. Even in the chill of this frosty day, snow making its way through my corner of the globe, I am basking in the warmth of His presence. I love you and am SO thankful beyond words or expression for you in so many ways.

xoxo j

From: Harry
To: Lorraine
Date: January 11, 2016 8:49 AM
Subject: Re: update: 11 complete, oh how sweet

Lorraine . . . I relate very closely to your recent experience and struggle with "letting go." In serious circumstances where things need to be precise and well thought through, it's so easy to fall into the trap of "control" and "self-reliance." When we release control, somehow we tend to feel that we're not doing "our job" right and get this strange idea that everything's gonna fall apart. The reality is, without Christ, we DO need to maintain complete control because we ARE in fact on our own. But with Christ we can be confident that He is there, not only to guide us, but to "fill in the gaps" when our abilities fall short. This is why we can "rest" in Him. It's a tough lesson to learn, and unfortunately it seems God is always having to lead me back to it (kicking and screaming I might add!).

I'm so happy to know that your white blood count is normal. It's always encouraging to see great results!

I hope you are having a great weekend! Greet Greg for me!
Harry

From: Lorraine
To: Harry
Date: January 11, 2016 8:59 AM
Subject: Re: Re: update: 11 complete, oh how sweet

Amen Harry!

It's something we all have to be reminded of. Sometimes we think we have already released control but the enemy comes in at those moments too, as he wants to plant thoughts that don't belong there. It is key to recognize these thoughts whether from ourselves in the form of pride or the enemy, and resist them and reject them immediately! God is so good!

I hope you are staying warm. So grateful for shelter from the cold and for the shelter of the Almighty!

Have a great day!

Lorraine

CHAPTER 22

Six More Pokes to Go!

From: Lorraine
To: All
Date: January 15, 2016 7:46 PM
Subject: Twelve went well . . . Six more pokes to go!

Hi everyone!

I hope this reaches all of you. After our computer fizzled out and we were forced to get a new one, I'm still trying to pull up my contacts and I'm on a learning curve.

Wednesday's chemo 12 went very well. My nurse was excellent, and when she inserted the IV, she said, "This is going to be nothin'." She was right! I barely felt a poke! I'm amazed that there has not been a single vein issue since my decision not to get the port. In awe! The remainder of the treatment went smoothly as well. Praise God! Now . . . only 6 more pokes to go!

I'm praying for my blood counts to remain in the normal range. My white counts were good this week. My red counts are a bit low, so I pray that they will return to normal as they have before.

I was able to get out and enjoy the warmer air and take a brisk walk today. I was very grateful to run into a couple of friends as I was out walking . . . one friend I haven't seen in several years. I was thinking about going in one direction but decided to take a different route and that's how we crossed paths! I marvel at the way God weaves things together to intersect at just the right moment! It's amazing how people come and go in the city but so wonderful when you haven't seen someone in a while and you pick up right where you left off. When we saw each other, we stopped with wide eyes of surprise. She screamed and literally picked me up in a big bear hug! We stood and chatted for a while as we caught up with each other and I filled her in on what I've been doing lately. She is a sweet woman of faith and a great encouragement to me and she quoted 1 Peter 2:24 (NIV): "'He himself bore our sins' in his body on the cross, so that we might die to sins and live for righteousness; 'by his wounds you have been healed.'"

I hope you all have a wonderful weekend. You remain in my prayers!

Love,
Lorraine/Rainie

"He himself bore our sins"
in his body on the cross,
so that we might die to sins
and live for righteousness;
"by his wounds
you have been healed."

1 PETER 2:24 NIV

From: Natalie
To: Lorraine
Date: January 16, 2016 8:52 AM
Subject: Re: Twelve went well . . . Six more pokes to go!

Woo hoo! Only 6 more—you've got this (and so does He). Prayers that your counts stay good so you can stay on track and get these behind you! Hugs and love to you.

xoxoxoxo Nat

From: Phyllis
To: Lorraine
Date: January 16, 2016 11:59 AM
Subject: Re: Twelve went well . . . Six more pokes to go!

Lorraine,

With every breath you take, God will be watching over you and will keep you in His constant care. Just wait on the Lord and you will get fresh strength, and before you know it, you'll be soaring like an eagle. ;)

Just love you. Know that your journey has kept me on my knees. And I thank you for that! Sending lots of hugs (handshakes spread too many germs—LOL—and I wouldn't want to get you sick before the next chemo).

Phyllis

From: Charlotte
To: Lorraine
Date: January 17, 2016 2:00 PM
Subject: Re: Twelve went well . . . Six more pokes to go!

Always be assured of my prayers! With your huge prayer circle, you will thrive!

Love,
Charlotte

From: Susie
To: Lorraine
Date: January 17, 2016 4:59 PM
Subject: Re: Twelve went well . . . Six more pokes to go!

Hi Rainie,

Thank God for your continued progress as you check these appointments off one by one. I'm so happy that you are responding so well to your treatments without all the horrible side effects. All I can say to that is God is good and has touched your body and soul and healed you already. He knows you are one of His precious angels because you have never doubted Him. Your faith is always constant in Him. I pray the last 6 pokes are as easy and that your levels continue to be normal.

I noticed today that the entire time I'm reading your emails, I'm smiling. My heart is full and I'm overjoyed for you and always waiting for a good update.

Love you, sweet little lady!
Xoxo

From: Jaime
To: Lorraine
Date: January 17, 2016 8:39 PM
Subject: Re: Twelve went well . . . Six more pokes to go!

Every praise report makes my spirit leap within!!! Praying for the red count and every single moment between now and poke #6. I love you, sister. I am with you fighting alongside you every step of the way!!!!

From: Patricia
To: Lorraine
Date: January 17, 2016 7:15 PM
Subject: Re: Twelve went well . . . Six more pokes to go!

Dear Lorraine,

Thank you for sending us your treatment updates. I feel they take all of us on your journey to success.

I thank Jesus and God our Father for seeing you through this time and giving you the courage to be grateful for the staff and treatments that are being provided for you.

We continue to pray for you.

In His Name,
Patricia

From: Shelly
To: Lorraine
Date: January 17, 2016 7:58 PM
Re: Twelve went well . . . Six more pokes to go!

Beautiful Lorraine -

God Bless You

Hope you sleep well and deep

Resting in His arms

From: Kathy S
To: Lorraine
Date: January 20, 2016 6:18 AM

Re: Twelve went well . . . Six more pokes to go!

Thank you for keeping us updated. What a wonderful encounter you had last week! Yes, "by his wounds you have been healed." You are His daughter, and He cares for you. Praying that you sense His closeness to you again today. I love you and of course He loves you deeply.

From: Mariellen
To: Lorraine
Date: January 20, 2016 9:09 PM
Subject: Chemo 12 is behind you!

Lorraine,

Praying for you tonight and asking our heavenly Father to bring full and absolute healing to you. Standing on God's Word in Matthew 7:7-11 (NIV): "Ask and it will be given to you; seek and you will find; knock and the door will be opened to you. For everyone who asks receives; the one who seeks finds; and to the one who knocks, the door will be opened. Which of you, if your son asks for bread, will give him a stone? Or if he asks for a fish, will give him a snake? If you, then, though you are evil, know how to give good gifts to your children, how much more will your Father in heaven give good gifts to those who ask him!"

You have been so faithful throughout this process! Praying that your faith will be sealed with God's unfailing love and blessing!

Love,
Mariellen

95

CHAPTER 23

No Pokes Today—
Another Delay

From: Lorraine
To: All
Date: January 21, 2016 9:47 AM
Subject: chemo 13 - no pokes today

Hi friends and family,

Still six more to go. I wasn't able to have treatment yesterday because my white count was too low for chemo. As you may recall, this happened right before Christmas and I was able to resume treatment the following week. So . . . we'll try again. Praying for all my blood counts to be completely normal! I plan on getting lots of rest this weekend and I'm looking forward to a successful and smooth chemo 13 next week! This delay puts my last treatment date at March 2nd. A little delay but we're still making great progress.

Have a great week everyone!

Love,
Lorraine

From: Sandy O
To: Lorraine
Date: January 21, 2016 6:51 PM
Subject: Re: chemo 13 - no pokes today

Sorry to hear that, Lorraine. I know that you like to keep your treatments on schedule. Maybe God wanted you to have a week off. ☺

From: Becky
To: Lorraine
Date: January 21, 2016 9:52 PM
Subject: Re: chemo 13 – no pokes today

Hi Lorraine, keep your head up. All things work out the way God wants. He loves you and He is there for you. Rest up and take care of yourself.

Xo Becky!

From: Lorraine
To: Becky
Date: January 22, 2016 8:46 AM
Subject: Re: Re: chemo 13 – no pokes today

Thank you Becky! I'll be resting my body as I rest IN HIM. Yes, He does love me and He loves you . . . and so do I! xoxo

Lorraine

From: Jean
To: Lorraine
Date: January 22, 2016 1:22 PM
Subject: Re: chemo 13 – no pokes today

So sorry, getting so close! Get plenty of rest! God is in charge!

XoXo Jean

From: Debby
To: Lorraine
Date: January 22, 2016 6:22 PM
Subject: Re: chemo 13 – no pokes today

Hello Dear Lorraine,

I'm glad your caregivers are keeping a close watch on things and are doing what's best for you. Praying that you have a restful week and for the white count to go back up by next week. Love you!

Hugs!
Debby

From: Mariellen
To: Lorraine
Date: January 22, 2016 6:51 PM
Subject: Re: chemo 13 – no pokes today

Ugh! Sorry to hear the final treatment date was pushed back! Glad you are resting, eating well, and getting ready for next week! We are praying for perfect numbers, and that they remain perfect throughout the rest of your treatment and beyond. You are doing so well, dear friend. You are in God's keeping. He will heal you and our faith will be multiplied by the love and grace He reveals through this process.

In full prayer mode for next week's treatment!

Love, MJ

From: Harry
To: Lorraine
Date: January 22, 2016 7:04 PM
Subject: Re: chemo 13 – no pokes today

Lorraine . . . I'm really marked by how much grace you show in the midst of the setbacks. It really speaks to your unflinching trust in the Lord. Only He knows the underlying reasons for the obstacles. They may just be a blessing in disguise! March really doesn't seem that far off . . . so in faith, we "march" on. :-) Have a wonderful weekend!

Harry

From: Lorraine
To: Harry
Date: January 22, 2016 8:13 PM
Subject: Re: Re: chemo 13 – no pokes today

Yes, we "march on"! In faith! I love it! I claim that one as mine. ;)

Thanks as always for your encouragement and prayers! Just a little bump in the road. I'm blessed as I see the beauty of good care I've been given and I'm grateful . . . so very grateful. God has me in the right place with the right people at the right time. I think about how quickly the weeks have passed since this all began in October and I realize the remainder of the weeks will go by even more quickly. Still six more . . . but ONLY six more!

Thanks, dear friend! Have a wonderfully blessed weekend!

Lorraine

From: Susie
To: Lorraine
Date: January 22, 2016 8:25 PM
Subject: Re: chemo 13 - no pokes today

Aw Rainie! I know you had to be disappointed . . . I'm sorry. I know how forward you are looking to having this behind you, but you must feel exhausted with your white blood count so low. But on the flip side God's working His miracle on His girl! :-) I'm feeling like this was His way of letting you know that He's healing you by bringing your levels down. Sometimes little setbacks are good things.

Love you and I'm praying that your levels return to normal and next week returns to normal so you can keep checking your calendar off.

Rest, pretty girl, and know that I love you so much. xoxo

From: Kathy B
To: Lorraine
Date: January 22, 2016 9:02 PM
Subject: Re: chemo 13 - no pokes today

Boo on those blood counts. It has to be frustrating to want to forge forward and then hit a temp bump in the road. Everything will be in alignment next week and you will be putting number 13 behind you for sure.

From: Missy
To: Lorraine
Date: January 22, 2016 9:40 PM
Subject: Re: chemo 13 - no pokes today

Six more! That is an easy countdown. Another delay, but perhaps a needed rest or respite. Even so, I know it is hard finding out when you are already all set to go. I hope you are still having good energy and are just resting for the white count. You are in my thoughts every day. Let me know when you want company again! Are you still taking photos? I don't recall seeing any recent ones. Another friend of mine takes a photo of sunrise over Lake Michigan every morning. Hmmm . . . sunrise . . . not really your thing! ☺

Love you, and hope this brings you a smile.
Missy

From: Lorraine
To: Missy
Date: January 22, 2016 9:53 PM
Subject: Re: Re: chemo 13 - no pokes today

Yes . . . just a little bump in the road. I realize how blessed I am to have excellent care as well as unlimited encouragement from you and all our family and friends!

Yes, my energy is good and I'm just resting up for next Wednesday. I'll certainly let you know if I can use some company again. I've been able to get later start times for the remainder of my appointments. It took some time and many requests but I finally got them moved.

Yes, I snap a few photos now and then. There is always something beautiful to see out this window . . . even the frozen lake is pretty. LOL—True . . . my body clock doesn't like to be up that early but I do love sunrises. In fact I have many in my collection since we've lived here. Sometimes the light wakes me up, so I'll jump out of bed, snap a few sunrise pics, then go back to bed. I'm always so happy to capture the beauty!

I hope you had a wonderful birthday! Love you!
Lorraine xoxo

Just a little note of encouragement to those who are going through a time like this: Remember to keep doing normal things . . . things that bring you pleasure . . . things that make you smile. Life is more than just this moment. Draw upon pleasant memories that make you smile . . . see the beauty in God's creation . . . capture moments in a photo lens, in your journal, etc. This difficult time does not have to rob you of good moments. A grateful heart invites God into your presence and brings breakthrough. Keep a balance and enjoy your life even during a difficult challenge.

CHAPTER 24

Chemo #13 Is Done!

From: Lorraine
To: All
Date: January 27, 2016 10:37 PM
Subject: Chemo 13 done!

Hi family & friends!

Chemo 13 was a success and we're counting down! My blood counts were excellent. Praise God! Five more to go!

It was a great day for a great day! The sun was shining brightly all day and we walked home in daylight! I love that it is staying light longer. I was happy to have a later start time for treatment . . . I feel much better overall when I don't have to be there very early in the morning. The remainder of my appointments are for later start times as well. An answered prayer! The downside of getting there later is the waiting room is very crowded. Actually it isn't a downside at all. I think God likes my appointments to be later . . . because a full waiting room makes for many more opportunities to pray . . . for a room filled with precious lives and stories of epic proportions. Every aspect of their stories is known by God. He sees the end from the beginning. I pray that somehow they all know this and trust Him as they take each step . . . in faith.

As I looked around, I imagined many different scenarios. Well, it's really not imagined . . . I've been through it and recognize the different expressions on those faces. I pray for all of them. I pray for the little woman with a cute wig and a walker, that she would be healed and no longer need that walker. I pray for the younger woman who is losing her hair and I remember what it felt like when I pulled out that clump of hair from my own head. I ask God to give her confidence as she walks forward on this journey.

There were several people in the waiting room today who seemed to be waiting to see the doctor, and I could tell by their body language that they were not sure what they would hear during their visit with him today. I've been there. I pray for them. A prayer for good news.

As the lab tech came out to call people in, she called some of these "veterans" by first name, not the number on their buzzers. Since I'm also a veteran after 13 weeks, I'm called by first name too. I address her by name too and we chitchat as she takes my blood. I never thought I'd say that I'm glad to be known by name in a chemo treatment center!

I pray for the lab techs and the lovely receptionists who check us in and the nurses, doctors, and aides . . . for wisdom and expertise in their jobs as well as loving hearts. I pray for every face I recall seeing and every face that is somehow now blurred in this memory of today's waiting room. I pray for transformed hearts by the renewing of their minds. I pray for healing. I pray for God's presence to be known to them all and that they would call upon the name of the Lord for their help and their salvation. I pray for the prayer warriors in my life . . . for the prayers of strength from the front lines on my behalf—faithful warriors, not "worriers." Prayers of belief and without doubt. I offer a prayer of gratitude!

My nurse was wonderful and it all went smoothly today! In the beginning there was a slight glitch. My pulse was rather high but it did come down to normal after some time to lie back and relax. My warriors had me covered and I rested . . . physically and in spirit . . . and I prayed . . . this time for myself.

Kathryn, one of my favorite nurses, did the IV beautifully. I told her that I love the way she comes to my window on the days when she is not my nurse and waves and smiles at me with the most joyful smile! She said,

"Well, I think you have lots of fans here."

I laughed and said, "Me? After the vein issues I had in the beginning?" She said, "Aww, that was nothing." So sweet! After all these weeks I've had the opportunity for some nice conversations with my nurses and trust has been built. I'm graced by the gift these women are giving me week after week and the gift God is giving me through this journey of healing.

I had quite a bit of "waiting" today . . . waiting for my appointments, waiting for lab results, waiting for my pulse to normalize, but each bit of pause was for a reason as God worked in my heart and I felt Him draw me closer. His peace calmed me, His power strengthened me, His love flooded me, His compassion worked through me, His joy comforted me.

I'm so thankful for each of you! You continue to encourage and love in such beautiful ways! I pray for blessings over you and that you will know His peace, strength, love, compassion, comfort, and joy as He draws you closer to Him in your "waiting room," whatever that might be.

Love to you all!
Lorraine/Rainie

From: Julie A
To: Lorraine
Date: January 28, 2016 9:32 AM
Subject: Re: Chemo 13 done!

Dear Lorraine,

Thank you for your faithful updates—you're rocking the communications, and in doing so, you are helping us all to better pray for you as we understand your needs, triumphs, and challenges.

God bless you for your witness to those at the hospital, be they staff or patients. It makes me sick that there are so many people getting cancer these days. How lovely for so many there to be on the receiving end of your prayers on their behalf. I will join you in that.

I have been praying for you and meditating on God's healing power in your life. The image of water comes to me all the time when I think of you. The ocean's waves washing to shore, bringing healing over you.

To the unbeliever, it must seem crazy when someone going through a serious health challenge is thankful, grateful, joyful, hopeful, prayerful, and peaceful. It must be hard to explain why God's grace and His promises to us are the very source of wellness rather than blaming Him for our situation. You have taught me so much and lifted me up in your trials, and I praise God for you, Lorraine.

Have a wonderful week. I'll have you in my thoughts and prayers.

Love,
Julie

From: Charlotte
To: Lorraine
Date: January 28, 2016 9:35 AM
Subject: Re: Chemo 13 done!

Lorraine,

Thank you so much for caring about others and writing!! This is simply beautiful and inspiring, Lorraine! The end of chemo is near, and so is a new beginning!

Love,
Charlotte

From: Missy
To: Lorraine
Date: January 28, 2016 7:40 AM
Subject: Re: Chemo 13 done!

This is so beautifully expressed. I see your spirit shining through. This one certainly brought tears to my eyes. You are so busy every moment you are there, caring for others. Thank you for sharing this glimpse. And so happy you are back on track!

Love,
Missy

From: Jane and Dan
To: Lorraine
Date: January 28, 2016 7:18 AM
Subject: Re: Chemo 13 done!

Dearest Rainie (& Greg!),

What a lovely, heartfelt update! It truly brought tears to my eyes. Thank you for drawing close to your heavenly Father during this time and for sharing that with all of us! May you know that your experience and responses are being followed and are going to transform the lives of others. God bless you!

We hold you both in our prayers as well as those others you encounter during your visits.

Love you so much!
Jane and Dan

From: Dan
To: Lorraine
Date: January 28, 2016 7:04 PM
Subject: Re: Chemo 13 done!

So happy to read your most recent update. Coming down the Home Stretch! As I read this, I couldn't help but think what a Spiritual Decathlon that you have been on. You are a Gold Medal winner in my book!

Luv you,
Dan & Jane

From: Christy
To: Lorraine
Date: January 31, 2016 9:48 AM
Subject: Re: Chemo 13 done!

I think about you often and pray for you on each and every occasion. I'm sending these well-wishes because Spring is fast approaching and new life, new growth, and God's love is unfolding right before our eyes in so many ways. ☺

From: Harry
To: Lorraine
Date: February 5, 2016 10:32 AM
Subject: Re: Chemo 13 done!

Lorraine . . . I just realized that I had not responded to your last update! Thank you for sharing that with us. Somehow I feel that every time I read an update from you, I'm having my devotions and alone time with God. It's so encouraging to see the many opportunities we have to bring God into each equation and lay it at His feet.

So often in our struggles we miss the opportunity to reach out to those who have similar or even tougher struggles. You and Joyce are my biggest examples of how God heals and lifts us as we reach out to those around us. Your updates are always a reminder that God is not only concerned about our needs, but the needs of all those others whose lives we touch.

Blessings!
Harry

... The prayer of

a righteous person

is powerful

and effective.

JAMES 5:16 NIV

As we go through struggles, whatever they may be, we should not forget that others are going through their own challenges. It might be health. It might be finances. It might be relational or spiritual or mental. Whatever it is, they need prayer too. Even though we desperately need prayer and encouragement for our situation, let's remember to pray for others as well. God will send His angels to hold up our arms with strength in order for us to lift up others through our offering of prayer as we intercede on their behalf.

> Therefore confess your sins to each other and pray for each other so that you may be healed. The prayer of a righteous person is powerful and effective. (James 5:16 NIV)

I love this scripture from the Amplified Bible version about love:

> Love bears all things [regardless of what comes], believes all things [looking for the best in each one], hopes all things [remaining steadfast during difficult times], endures all things [without weakening]. (1 Corinthians 13:7 AMP)

This so accurately describes the love flowing into my life from the beautiful people who have been steadfast during my difficulty and enduring alongside me, staying strong, and infusing strength into me with their words and other acts of kindness!

May the LOVE (which is God) keep you in "fadeless hope" at all times, no matter what you are facing and keep you ever ready to believe the best . . . without weakness!

CHAPTER 25

Four More and Out the Door

From: Lorraine
To: All
Date: February 5, 2016 12:58 PM
Subject: short update . . . chemo 14

Four more and out the door! ☺

Hi everyone!

I'll make this one short and sweet . . . which is pretty much what chemo 14 was. The day went quickly and smoothly . . . praise God!

There were many blessings to count throughout the day, from the first morning greeting of a new day and the sun sparkling over the lake outside my window to meeting a lovely woman in the waiting room who was also there for her infusion appointment, a pleasant walk to and from treatment, and answered prayers for normal white blood counts!

I'm enormously grateful for God's mercy and the fact that we are now in the home stretch. Next Wednesday is chemo 15.

Thank you so much, as always, for your encouragement, prayers, and love! I hope you all have a great weekend!

Love,
Lorraine/Rainie

From: Mariellen
To: Lorraine
Date: February 6, 2016 10:52 AM
Subject: Re: short update . . . chemo 14

Lorraine! This is really great news! You are almost done! A month from today we will be celebrating the end of your chemo, God's mercy, and the beautiful and grace-filled way you have navigated this trial.

We continue to pray for you every day and are looking forward to celebrating your good health!

Love, Mariellen

From: Susie
To: Lorraine
Date: February 6, 2016 2:53 PM
Subject: Re: short update . . . chemo 14

Rainie . . . "Praise God" is right! Oh goodness, you are so blessed and I am so grateful for His healing hands. This is just the news I wait to hear every week.

You enjoy your weekend, precious girl, and know that you are never far from my heart and my constant prayers! I love you!!

Big hugs to you and I am counting them down with you,
Sus

From: Kathy B
To: Lorraine
Date: February 7, 2016 12:03 PM
Subject: Re: short update . . . chemo 14

Rainie,

Your upbeat attitude through this whole process never ceases to amaze me. Thanks for being an inspiration to me.

Love you . . .

From: Kathy S
To: Lorraine
Date: February 10, 2016 6:02 AM
Subject: Re: short update . . . chemo 14

Lorraine,

Another Wednesday . . . I thank Almighty God, our Father, for you in my life! And the opportunity to lift your face, your heart, your body to Him. As you have taught me, He is your nurse, your physician, your comforter, your strength-giver! He knows the end from the beginning (that is again a good reminder for me) and He promises: "I will not leave you as orphans; I will come to you" (John 14:18 NIV), and "Peace I leave with you; my peace I give you . . . " (John 14:27 NIV).

You are amazing, Lorraine, and God loves you so much! Thank you for your encouragement and wisdom that you have shared with me. I have needed it so much and I am very grateful for your prayers in faith. I am trusting that God is blessing you today each step of the way . . . again.

I love you,
Kathy

"I will not leave
you as orphans;
I will come to you."

JOHN 14:18 NIV

CHAPTER 26

Three More to Go!

From: Lorraine
To: All
Date: February 13, 2016 7:42 PM
Subject: quick update . . . 3 more to go!

Hi everyone!

Chemo 15 was very smooth and there were many blessings wrapped up in the gift of the day! Three more to go! I'm so thankful! Praying for normal white blood counts for the remaining treatments.

I hope you all have a sweet weekend! Happy Valentine's Day! xoxo

Love,
Lorraine/Rainie

From: Sandy O
To: Lorraine
Date: February 14, 2016 6:57 AM
Subject: Re: quick update . . . 3 more to go!

Woow!!! What a blessing to have only 3 more!!! I can remember the very beginning of this journey. God has been in control of this all the way, and you have given Him the glory!!! He is delighting in you, Lorraine!

Love you!
Sandy

From: Julie A
To: Lorraine
Date: February 14, 2016, 7:35 AM
Subject: Re: quick update . . . 3 more to go!

Such fantastic news. I have been thinking of you and praying for you all week. Lord bless you this week. Three more! Hip hip hooray!

> The Lord is my light and my salvation—whom shall I fear? (Psalm 27:1 NIV)

Julie

From: Kathy B
To: Lorraine
Date: February 13, 2016 8:25 PM
Subject: Re: quick update . . . 3 more to go!

DOING MY HAPPY DANCE!!!!!!!!!

From: Becky
To: Lorraine
Date: February 13, 2016 10:07 PM
Subject: Re: quick update . . . 3 more to go!

Glad to hear! You're in the home stretch! Happy Valentine's Day to you and Greg!

From: Harry
To: Lorraine
Date: February 14, 2016 7:28 AM
Subject: Re: quick update . . . 3 more to go!

Wonderful news! Nice gift to wake up to on a Sunday morning! It's hard to believe you're almost there, Lorraine! We'll be praying that the remaining treatments (empowered by prayer) will bring COMPLETE healing and FINAL closure!

Happy Valentine's Day!
Harry ☺

113

From: Melissa
To: Lorraine
Date: February 14, 2016 3:00 PM
Subject: Re: quick update . . . 3 more to go!

You're almost there!! I keep praying for all to go smoothly, and for the resulting effect in your body to be full, complete, and permanent healing, dear sister! May it be so to you, in Jesus's most precious, holy, and powerful name!! Love you!!!

From: Missy
To: Lorraine
Date: February 14, 2016 1:33 PM
Subject: Re: quick update . . . 3 more to go!

Always waiting to hear, and I am so pleased it went so well. The big countdown!

Love you. Hope you and Greg are having a lovely Valentine's Day.

From: Susie
To: Lorraine
Date: February 15, 2016 7:10 PM
Subject: Re: quick update . . . 3 more to go!

Hi Sweet Rainie,

I love receiving your updates!!

I am also praying for normal white blood counts for the remainder of your treatments. I'm counting down your treatments right along with you and praying so hard every step of the way. God is listening to each and every one of us, and I truly believe you're already cured from this horrible cancer. I just know it!!

I hope you had a sweet Valentine's Day with your love!!

I love you!!!
xoxo Sus

From: Lorraine
To: Susie
Date: February 15, 2016 9:25 PM
Subject: Re: Re: quick update . . . 3 more to go!

I believe it too Sus! Thank you for your faithful prayers and believing without a single doubt! You are beautiful!

I'm glad you are back home safely! I hope you're feeling great!!!

I love you so much!
Rainie xoxo

CHAPTER 27

Two . . . Wahoo!

From: Lorraine
To: All
Date: February 18, 2016 10:10 PM
Subject: Two . . . Wahoo!

Hi friends and family!

TWO MORE TO GO!!!

Treatment 16 went very well. My white blood count was just a bit low but still safe for chemo, so treatment was given. I feel good. I'll be trying to rest up as much as possible and keep eating healthy to bring the count up again.

My visit with the oncologist went well. He said I'm doing great. Two weeks after my final visit I will have a scan. My prayer is that it is free and clear to reveal my healing!!!

My cancer marker blood test (CA125) came down from 11.4 to 7.4. Hallelujah! 7 is certainly a great number! Normal range is 0-30. I still want a zero! ☺

Thanks for your prayers and continued words of encouragement. I love hearing from you. Have a wonderful weekend!

Love,
Lorraine/Rainie

From: Dave
To: Lorraine
Date: February 19, 2016 8:29 AM
Subject: Re: Two . . . Wahoo!

Lorraine,

This is great news!!

You are such a trooper and you certainly have been an inspiration to me!

Blessings!!
Dave

From: Krista
To: Lorraine
Date: February 19, 2016 9:07 AM
Subject: Re: Two . . . Wahoo!

Wonderful News!! We continue to think about you both and keep you in our prayers!

Love, Krista, Brian, Lily, and Mason

From: Judy
To: Lorraine
Date: February 19, 2016 9:07 AM
Subject: Re: Two . . . Wahoo!

Hello Lorraine,

I am so glad you are doing well and pray that you will feel well after the treatments too. I have been praying that your follow-up scan would show zero traces of cancer. (Great minds think alike.)

Praying the Lord will carry you through these last treatments and touch you with His healing hand to totally "erase" any signs of cancer in your body—for now and in the future.

I don't know if you have the time/energy, but I sure would like it if we could get together for lunch again and catch up. Mondays won't work for me, but any other day. You can wait and write when you have a day in mind.

Love you dear Lorraine! Judy

From: Shelly
To: Lorraine
Date: February 19, 2016 10:00 AM
Subject: Re: Two . . . Wahoo!

Oh Lorraine what a ride! I sure hope today you feel the wind at your back. Such a glorious day. ☺ We love you!

From: Rev. Bill
To: Lorraine
Date: February 19, 2016 5:32 PM
Subject: Re: Two . . . Wahoo!

That is wonderful and encouraging news! I am so happy for you and thankful to the Lord.

For His glory,
Bill

From: Debby
To: Lorraine
Date: February 20, 2016 8:31 AM
Subject: Re: Two . . . Wahoo!

Such good news, Lorraine! Only two more treatments, praise God! I'll be praying for that zero!

Love you!

From: Lorraine
To: Debby
Date: February 20, 2016 1:55 PM
Subject: Re: Re: Two . . . Wahoo!

Thank you so much Debby! You have been on this journey with me every step of the way and your faithful prayers have lifted me up!

I know you will pray in firm, steadfast faith for the revealing of the healing God has already done! Your words have given me encouragement and your generosity has blessed me with tangible gifts, and when I look at the things you've sent me, I see your beautiful smile!

I am still amazed at how God brought us together! Wow! We are so blessed! I'm so grateful for my sisters in Christ and I thank the Lord for you constantly and pray for favor over you and your family.

Praying also for your health, sweet sis!

Love you!
Lorraine xoxo

From: Harry
To: Lorraine
Date: February 20, 2016 4:02 PM
Subject: Re: Two . . . Wahoo!

AMEN Sister!!! Great news here! We're all running with you across that finish line! Can't wait to hear the confirmation of what we all know God has already done!

Harry

CHAPTER 28

Down on My Knees

A very strange thing happened to me on my way into treatment #16. I arrived at the hospital and was approaching the elevator in the lobby when suddenly it felt as if both of my feet were yanked right out from under me in less than a split second. I fell flat onto both knees on the marble floor. Thankfully I was wearing my full-length down coat, which most likely buffered the impact. I heard a few gasps from the several people who rushed from all around to ask if I was OK.

I replied, "I'm not sure. It was so fast that I need a moment to process what just happened!"

A gentleman helped me up as I brushed myself off. I told all the concerned people who were so kind to stop that I was fine and I thanked them all.

I checked the bottom of my shoes and there was no ice . . . no water—they were completely dry. I didn't see anything wet on the floor either.

I immediately went into warrior mode and said to myself, "It looks like the devil is trying to keep me from treatment! Well . . . that's not gonna happen! I will not let anything stop me and I rebuke the enemy right now in Jesus's name!" I asked the Lord for His favor, for no bruising, swelling, or pain. By the time I was called in for my treatment session, I'd almost forgotten about it. I relaxed and received my treatment . . . pain free!

Whenever something like that strikes, I say, "Something good is about to happen." Something good did happen! With an excellent drop in the CA125 cancer marker number . . . the blood count being in a zone in which I could receive treatment . . . my doctor saying that I'm doing great . . . not to mention all the conversations I was able to have with nurses, patients, aides, etc.—I would say many good things happened!

One little nursing aide was going to be leaving for a job closer to her home. I took her a note with a gift card to say good-bye and thanked her for her kindness to me, and we shared a tender hug. We had a deep conversation because she opened up to me freely. She stayed in my chemo room for quite some time, sharing so much of her story! We talked about God, and when we did, tears streamed down her face. I shared as much as I could about my relationship with Jesus in the less-than-private space we had. I could tell that she has a hunger for God. I pray for her and her two children. She is a single parent. I pray for their protection and that God will send more believers into her life to share the gospel and bring her into a true and right relationship with Him. I pray for transformed hearts and for the renewing of their minds—and of everyone I meet! I'm so thankful for such a wonderful day that ended so well!

Oh . . . and I remain bruise free and have no swelling or pain. Praise God!

"Lord, you are my refuge!" Because you chose the Most High as your dwelling place, no evil will fall upon you, and no affliction will approach your tent, for he will command his angels to protect you in all your ways. With their hands they will lift you up so you will not trip over a stone. (Psalm 91:9-12 ISV)

As I recap this journey, I feel the relief all over again that the chemo sessions were drawing to a close. It is a reminder that the trials we go through are not forever. There is an end to the treatment! We might have to go through a valley to get to the other side, but there IS another side we are going toward as we forge ahead! The treatment was a great lesson for me in many ways. It was certainly a lesson of learning to trust . . . really trust. It was also a fascinating eye-opener—to see through the eyes of faith as God kept His promise to never leave me nor forsake me and to remember:

Now faith is the substance of things hoped for, the evidence of things not seen. (Hebrews 11:1 KJV)

 He rescued us from so great a threat of death, and will continue to rescue us. On Him we have set our hope. And He will again rescue us [from danger and draw us near]. . . . (2 Corinthians 1:10 AMP)

CHAPTER 29

One...

From: Lorraine
To: All
Date: February 25, 2016 7:00 PM
Subject: ONE . . .

One . . . more . . . to go!!!

Yesterday went very well. No issues . . . a smooth and successful treatment.

My hemoglobin is down a bit so it is my specific prayer that my hemoglobin comes up to normal quickly as it has before. My white count was pretty good but I pray for it to come up even more.

There were so many blessings yesterday . . . almost too many to count. First thing in the morning, as is the case each week, I have several texts from my soul sisters (prayer warriors) checking on me and letting me know they are with me in spirit and in prayer. I also receive a text from my bff soul sister of over 30 years who sends me a photo of her hand, ringing a special copper bell that hangs just outside her door on her ranch in Texas. She prays for me and then rings the bell as an Amen! There is just something so sweet and special about the thought of my dear friend who is really more of a sister . . . praying for me and ringing that bell . . . for me! It touches me deeply.

As I was leaving the building, I rushed outdoors to get a cab because it was snowing and blowing like crazy. I was in a hurry because I wasn't sure how long it would take to get a cab. Usually the doorman comes out and helps me but he was talking to two women at the desk, so I simply asked him for a cab light. I saw a cab waiting in front under our canopy, but it was waiting for someone else who had ordered it. As soon as I stepped away from it, my doorman came rushing out to help me and began to lead me to that same cab. I said, "No, no, that was ordered by someone else." He said, "No, this is your cab!" and proceeded to open the door. A woman had followed my doorman out and said to the cab driver, "I'm Annie and this is my cab but I'm giving it to her. Please take her wherever she wants to go, and it is paid for by me." As she was saying this, my doorman was practically swooping me up and putting me inside! I had tears in my eyes as I thanked them, and as the cab pulled away, I had my hand on the window, still saying "Thank you!" They were standing there waving back at me and smiling, like angels! I got to the hospital with plenty of time to spare, still overjoyed because of that loving woman . . . Annie! Of all names . . . Annie . . . is my mom's name. She is in heaven but I know she would have done the exact same thing!

I had some great conversations with nurses and aides and a quick but very deep conversation with the lab tech! She is beautiful. We talked about our faith and about forgiveness and love and how important it is to walk in love, and that it is not a suggestion but a command from God to love others as He first loved us. It all began with my telling her about the blessing I had just received with the cab, and this led her to begin telling me about the blessings in her life. We connected! We hugged! I was also blessed by that encounter!

My "favorite" nurse came in to say hi as I was waiting for my labs to come back and getting set up in my room. She is young, excellent, and sweet, and one of the best with the IV too. She is the one who walks past my room on the days she is not my nurse and smiles at me with that big, expressive, joyful smile. She is such a doll. I told her that next week is my last week. I said, "I don't know who my nurse will be on my final week, but I'm hoping it's you." She said, "Well, I just might be able to arrange that." Oh boy! I told her it would certainly be a great way to celebrate. ☺ When my chemo was finished and I was waiting for Greg to arrive, I was walking to the bathroom and she was down the hall. She said, "We're all set. I'll see you next week." I did a little happy dance and blew her a kiss!

There were so many other blessings. I won't overwhelm you now with a lengthy list but just to say . . . keep your eyes on Him and you WILL see the blessings all around you.

I feel good today . . . a blessing! The snow stopped yesterday just before it was time for Greg and me to walk home . . . another blessing!

I'm sooooo grateful that next Wednesday is my last treatment . . . a huge blessing!

Thank you all for your love, encouragement, and prayers! Blessings!

Love,
Lorraine/Rainie

From: Carol/Samantha
To: Lorraine
Date: February 26, 2016 6:53 AM
Subject: Re: ONE . . .

Sis, I am so very proud of you! You have gone through this situation with such Grace. You have touched so many people through your journey. More than you will ever know.

I am sitting in bed with a cup of coffee and my 4 dogs, crying because your encounter with Annie touched my heart! God is so amazing! He puts Angels in our lives at times we would not expect. I wish everyone realized that we are all supposed to love each other and help each other. Our world would be so much better off.

You are truly Blessed, my Friend, in so many ways! I am so thrilled that this part of your journey is almost done!

Enjoy the weekend! I love you, my Friend!
Your Sis!

From: Lorraine
To: Carol/Samantha
Date: February 26, 2016 1:17 PM
Subject: Re: Re: ONE . . .

I was reflecting on how we met. Do you remember the exact year? Early 80s. I remember you coming by my booth when we were at a trade show and we talked and started going to lunch together, etc. Our friendship blossomed so naturally. It was meant to be! You were so sweet and loving then and you are now!

I agree with you about how our world would be so much better if everyone realized that we are supposed to love each other and help each other. It would be heaven in that case, I suppose. But . . . people like Annie, and others who have stepped out of the shadows to bless, have shown me that good people do still exist in this world and there is hope. People like you who shine your light and positive attitude and love, give hope to everyone you touch. You have certainly blessed me, my bff . . . now and throughout the years! Your love is a gift! A huge gift from God!

My cousin who is praying for me loved the story of your bell and how you ring it for me as you pray for me every day. She said, "I'm always praying for you. I wish I had a bell though. ;)" I told her that you also sent me one as a sweet gift and that I can't wait until Greg and I find a place to hang it up and ring it for everyone too!

I love you sis! Rainie xoxoxo

From: Michael
To: Lorraine
Date: February 26, 2016 6:49 AM
Subject: Re: ONE . . .

Lorraine,

All the angels in one's life are always there when you least expect them. ☺ All my best to one who truly deserves it. All our love and thanks to God for His help for you.

Michael

From: Mary
To: Lorraine
Date: February 26, 2016 4:50 AM
Subject: Re: ONE . . .

Praise the Lord! I love watching how the Lord is so sweetly watching over you! People are really good. We just need to notice it more, as you do. These little sweet kindnesses are kisses from God. Praise the Lord. This IS your last chemo . . . forever and ever. Amen.

Mary

From: Aunt Betty and Uncle Orville
To: Lorraine
Date: February 26, 2016 5:13 PM
Subject: Re: ONE . . .

Dear Greg and Rainie,

Soooo glad it's down to one! Our plan for Palm Sunday is to celebrate Rainie's long journey and its fulfillment. All of us have experienced the answers to our prayers for her. God is good. Learned that in Sunday school and have seen evidence all my life. You are not asked to bring anything edible to the brunch. It is our intention that we CELEBRATE our having Rainie back in our circle. She is to be our Queen for a day. Do wear your crown!

Big Bunches of Love
Aunt Betty and Uncle Orville

From: Lorraine
To: Aunt Betty and Uncle Orville
Date: February 27, 2016 5:13 PM
Subject: Re: Re: ONE . . .

Oh my! You are so sweet and thoughtful and loving. I so look forward to seeing you all and celebrating, not only the answers to our prayers, but celebrating the Easter season, which is the greatest reminder of His grace!

I might not be able to wear an actual crown, but I will wear my halo. Missy knows what this means. ;) I'll have to keep my hat on all day. I have two "halos" that are just the sides of the hair on a band to be worn under hats. ;)

That said . . . In Christ we are all princes and princesses—sons and daughters of the Most High King! Crowned with victory! I'll be honored to sit at the table with you!

I love you all so very much!

Rainie

From: Kathy B
To: Lorraine
Date: February 27, 2016 7:34 AM
Subject: Re: ONE . . .

As always, this update made me cry, but even more so when I read the part about Annie, as I did not need a reminder it was your mom's name. She was shining down on you for sure.

Fingers crossed for good counts and smooth sailing through the week.

Love You . . .
Kathy

From: Kate
To: Lorraine
Date: February 27, 2016 9:37 AM
Subject: Re: ONE . . .

Lorraine!!

This such good news!! Closing in on completing this part of your journey! So many beautiful blessings on your path . . .

You're truly an inspiration of Courage, Strength, Love, and Grace . . .

So special of your friend to pray and ring the copper bell for all the angels to hear.

I will continue to pray for you my friend . . . and that all readings of tests come up to where they're supposed to be . . . and that the sunshine & warmth of today will be a reminder of His Hope.

Sending hugs of reassurance that God has you in His care . . .

xoxo's,
-Kate, One of Your Prayer Warriors :-)

From: Kathy S
To: Lorraine
Date: February 27, 2016 11:37 AM
Subject: Re: ONE . . .

Lovely, Loving Lorraine!

Thank you so much for sending me your emails with every detail that you send. It means so much to me and helps me so much! It builds into my faith for my own personal challenges and journey . . . and it reveals how God is answering prayers along the way specifically said for you and your journey. Yes, I definitely had tears in my eyes as I was reading your email. It is such a joy to read about God's faithfulness and how he is involved in the details of our lives! The fact that the wonderful generous lady's name was Annie . . . your mother's name . . . what a precious God and Creator we have. He knows His plans for you. He knows the END from the beginning! It is a joy to join you in prayer. Thank you for inviting me! Thank you for praying for me as well! The hurdles are getting smaller. I am learning in a deeper way to count God's power to be made perfect in my weakness. Where else will I go?

Thank you for being my sister in Christ in a very real and powerful way!

I love you!
Kathy

From: Laurie
To: Lorraine
Date: February 28, 2016 10:18 AM
Subject: Re: ONE . . .

And my prayer is that next Wednesday is your last treatment. Period.

What a wonderful attitude and spirit you have . . .

From: Christie
To: Lorraine
Date: February 29, 2016 10:18 AM
Subject: Re: ONE . . .

You were the first thing on my mind when my eyes opened this morning.

From: Gail
To: Lorraine
Date: March 1, 2016 8:21 PM
Subject: Re: ONE . . .

Dear Lorraine,

We are hoping and praying that your numbers are excellent for your last che-motherapy tomorrow. You have embraced this entire experience in your won-derfully loving and caring ways. We will really rejoice when this last treatment is behind you! Will have you in our hearts . . .

Love, Gail and Michael too!

From: Kathy S
To: Lorraine
Date: March 2, 2016 6:05 AM
Subject: Re: ONE . . .

Wednesday! #18!!!

Thank You, Father, for Your love and faithfulness to Lorraine.

Let today be triumphant in the name of Jesus! Cover all the details as You have every step of the way. You know her needs before she asks and she is Yours! Thank You for loving her the way that You do and being the God who hears and answers prayers! Nothing is too big or too small for You, and You know the end from the beginning.

Thank You, Father, in the name of Jesus.

How grateful I am to have been able to ride on the wings of faith and the prayers of faithful witnesses to my journey! How amazing our God is—knowing exactly what each one of us needs and just waiting for us to ask Him for it. His love never fails. His power—the same power that raised Jesus from the dead—is available to each of us if we would only ask!

> Therefore, since we are surrounded by so great a cloud of witnesses [who by faith have testified to the truth of God's absolute faithfulness], stripping off every unnecessary weight and the sin which so easily and cleverly entangles us, let us run with endurance and active persistence the race that is set before us, [looking away from all that will distract us and] focusing our eyes on Jesus, who is the Author and Perfecter of faith [the first incentive for our belief and the One who brings our faith to maturity], who for the joy [of accomplishing the goal] set before Him endured the cross, disregarding the shame, and sat down at the right hand of the throne of God [revealing His deity, His authority, and the completion of His work]. Just consider and meditate on Him who endured from sinners such bitter hostility against Himself [consider it all in comparison with your trials], so that you will not grow weary and lose heart. (Hebrews 12:1-3 AMP)

And the same passage again, but this time from The Message Bible:

> Do you see what this means—all these pioneers who blazed the way, all these veterans cheering us on? It means we'd better get on with it. Strip down, start running—and never quit! No extra spiritual fat, no parasitic sins. Keep your eyes on Jesus, who both began and finished this race we're in. Study how he did it. Because he never lost sight of where he was headed—that exhilarating finish in and with God—he could put up with anything along the way: Cross, shame, whatever. And now he's there, in the place of honor, right alongside God. When you find yourselves flagging in your faith, go over that story again, item by item, that long litany of hostility he plowed through. That will shoot adrenaline into your souls! (Hebrews 12:1-3 MSG)

And one final passage to leave you with for this chapter:

> Holding forth the word of life; that I may rejoice in the day of Christ, that I have not run in vain, neither laboured in vain. (Philippians 2:16 KJV)

CHAPTER 30

Chemo Complete— Wednesday Was Sweet!

From: Lorraine
To: All
Date: March 4, 2016 6:36 PM
Subject: chemo complete . . .

Chemo complete . . . Wednesday was sweet!

It has been quite a journey . . .

I feel great and I'm extremely happy to be finished with EIGHTEEN WEEKS of chemo! Twenty weeks actually, if we count the two delays due to low white blood counts. At the beginning of this, I had no idea that the time would go by so quickly, but God in His great mercy and grace made the time fly by.

God has blessed me in so many beautiful ways, and through so many beautiful people and has allowed me to see the goodness and depth of love that exists in the hearts of those who care . . . those who love! To be loved by so many people is a heart-melting, humbling experience . . . an honor, a privilege, an inexplicable blessing . . . truly from the hand of God.

My heart leapt with delight every time I received a note of encouragement, flowers, gifts, cards, emails, texts . . . with words of love and faith-filled prayers that lifted my spirit and kept me strong. Each of you with your own special way of showing unconditional love to a friend/sister/cousin/aunt! Your love has been a gift and it continues to bless me!

My heart is leaping with gladness again today as I'm celebrating this accomplishment. Wednesday was very, very sweet. I had visits with the nurses and huge hugs from each of them. My doctor even stopped in to give me a hug. He said his fingers are crossed for my CT scan to come back all clear. I thanked him and said, "Pray!" He nodded in affirmation. My CT scan will be March 16th. Thank you for continuing to lift me up to the Lord for my CT scan to reveal NO cancer!

I thank the Lord for each of you and keep you in my prayers! God bless you richly!

"The Lord bless you and keep you; the Lord make his face shine on you and be gracious to you; the Lord turn his face toward you and give you peace."
(Numbers 6:24-26 NIV)

With Much Love,
Lorraine/Rainie

From: Harry
To: Lorraine
Date: March 4, 2016 6:55 PM
Subject: Re: chemo complete . . .

Lorraine! This is absolutely amazing! I think we're all stunned at how fast this treatment seemed to fly by! I'm completely ambushed when I think about how much grace and peace God has given you through this whole process. I know I speak for every one of us when I tell you how grateful I am that you invited us into your journey with the Great Physician. The testimonies and insights have been so uplifting and faith restoring! OK . . . so 12 days more could feel like a lifetime when you have to wait for test results . . . but I'm confident God will keep the momentum going!

Prayers for your heart to "be still" as you rest in expectation!

Rejoicing with you!
Harry

From: Charlotte
To: Lorraine
Date: March 4, 2016 7:39 PM
Subject: Re: chemo complete . . .

Congratulations, Lorraine! You made it through, as I knew you would.

My prayers continue every day. Your scan will be clear.

I hope you are up to doing something relaxing and fun this weekend. Sunday will be a mild day. Please enjoy it. It's almost spring, and a new season for you. A new season of living and good health.

Much love and peace,
Charlotte

From: Bruce and Sandy
To: Lorraine
Date: March 4, 2016 7:40 PM
Subject: Re: chemo complete . . .

YES!! Such blessed news, Lorraine!

And we will pray for a good test on 3/16.

The Lord bless you and keep you . . .
Bruce and Sandy

From: Natalie
To: Lorraine
Date: March 4, 2016 7:44 PM
Subject: Re: chemo complete . . .

So many prayers coming your way! YOU DID IT! Chemo is done . . . spring is right around the corner and you are ready to enjoy ☺.

Hugs and kisses from my mom and me!!!!

From: Shannon
To: Lorraine
Date: March 5, 2016 2:53 AM
Subject: Re: chemo complete . . .

Dearest Lorraine,

I pray for you every day and I hope you can feel the love I have for you. You're such a blessing to every life you touch.

Words seem to fail me, but I just wanted you to know that you're in my thoughts, my prayers, and my heart every day.

Your sister in Christ
Shannon ♡

From: Jaime
To: Lorraine
Date: March 6, 2016 10:59 AM
Subject: Re: chemo complete . . .

GOD IS SO GOOD! I thank Him for this journey, and all He accomplished through you in the lives of others!!! I hope you have a wonderful time of celebration. You deserve it!!!!

- xoxoxo j

From: Kathy S
To: Lorraine
Date: March 6, 2016 12:48 PM
Subject: Re: chemo complete . . .

Lorraine,

I am so grateful for all the ways . . . & I'm sure I don't even know all the ways . . . that our God has been faithful to you! Thank you for all the details that you have shared with us . . . the lady giving you her cab, the man who lifted you into the cab, all the days you didn't need a cab because you could walk, the right nurses at the right time. I thank God for His loving care of you. Know that it has been a true encouragement to me. He is more than faithful!

Much love,
Kathy

From: Sandy O
To: Lorraine
Date: March 8, 2016 7:13 AM
Subject: Re: chemo complete . . .

Hi Lorraine!

Tomorrow will be your 1st free Wednesday in 20 weeks!!! Hope that you are enjoying your time off from treatments!!!

Praying for your scan on the 16th . . .

Love you!
Sandy

From: Kathy S
To: Lorraine
Date: March 9, 2016 5:35 AM
Subject: Re: chemo complete . . .

Lorraine ~ Wednesday—NO CHEMO!!!!!

Thanking God! Love you & Greg!

Kathy

From: Susie
To: Lorraine
Date: March 9, 2016 11:58 AM
Subject: Re: chemo complete . . .

Hi Rainie,

I completely understand being emotional. You have every right! You've come through quite an ordeal but with God's healing mercy you have been healed from this horrible disease. Don't allow the "enemy" to place any doubt in your mind. That's exactly what he wants you to feel but you are so much bigger than he is. You are blessed beyond measure and are a True Woman of Faith!

God won't let you down. He's touched your body, mind, and soul and will fight the enemy off for you. I continue praying for your complete recovery and believe with all my heart that you have been healed.

I love, love, love you!

Please know that through the tests the enemy throws at us, we become stronger. You are stronger than most and certainly more blessed than most. God will hold you in His arms and protect you.

Xoxo Sus

From: Lorraine
To: Susie
Date: March 9, 2016 12:42 PM
Subject: Re: Re: chemo complete . . .

Thank you Sus!

Amen to everything you've said! I appreciate your being my cheerleader on this journey and for speaking the truth! Your encouragement means the world to me and gives me strength.

We all have battles; just different battles at different times. I will keep my armor on, and as God sets His angels' special charge over me, I will win battles I do not even have to fight. You too, sister in Christ! No matter how big or small, we are more than conquerors in Christ Jesus!

You are a powerhouse! A sweet, loving, kind, yet bold and courageous powerhouse! Stay strong!

I love you so much!

I hope you're enjoying the weekend. I was trying clothes and hats on to see what I want to pack for our little trip. We decided to go to St. Augustine for a few days right after Palm Sunday and be back in time for Easter. ☺

You are beautiful in every way!

Love,
Rainie xoxo

From: Kathy B
To: Lorraine
Date: March 9, 2016 2:11 PM
Subject: Re: chemo complete . . .

Doing my happier-than-happy dance. And fingers crossed for a clean bill of health.

—Kathy

From: Lorraine
To: Kathy B
Date: March 9, 2016 3:33 PM
Subject: Re: Re: chemo complete . . .

AMEN!!! Happy dancing here too! ☺

It's strange, though, the feeling you get after you finish. As happy as I am, it's like withdrawal. My friend Jaime said it is probably similar to what Olympic athletes go through after they reach their goal. It's like you run on adrenaline for such a long time, completely focused, then you are placed back into real life and you need to adjust again. It was mostly over the weekend that it felt a little odd.

I'm so happy that this is the first Tuesday night that I won't have to swallow down those three steroids they make you take the night before treatment, and Wednesday I won't be taking that same worn path. Wow! I can relax and enjoy not having to go to chemo!

Hope you're having a good week.

Love you! Rainie

From: Kathy B
To: Lorraine
Date: March 9, 2016 4:09 PM
Subject: Re: Re: chemo complete . . .

Let it be known that I am still here . . . and I am not going anywhere!

From: Lorraine
To: Kathy B
Date: March 9, 2016 4:56 PM
Subject: Re: Re: chemo complete . . .

Aww, I know you are here and I know you are not going anywhere! You've been here ever since we met . . . my first friend in life! Wow! What is it now, 54 years? Amazing! ☺

I love you!
Rainie

 Sweet friendships refresh the soul and awaken our hearts with joy, for good friends are like the anointing oil that yields the fragrant incense of God's presence. (Proverbs 27:9 TPT)

 So encourage each other and build each other up, just as you are already doing. (1 Thessalonians 5:11 NLT)

 A friend loves at all times. . . . (Proverbs 17:17a NKJV)

Friendship . . . is the instrument by which God reveals to each the beauties of all the others. (C. S. Lewis, *The Four Loves*)

Looking back over all of the emails sent over the course of my treatment, I am amazed at how quickly the time went as I view it from this side of the mountain! It truly was a mountain that came upon me from out of nowhere. A startling slap in the face! I had to get my armor on and go to war!

Friendship . . .

is the instrument

by which God reveals

to each the beauties

of all the others.

C. S. LEWIS, *THE FOUR LOVES*

I realize that it wasn't my strength but the strength of Almighty God, who does fight our battles. His Word says that He is the Conqueror and those who have a relationship with Him have His Spirit living inside their hearts; therefore we are conquerors too. The scripture says that we are more than conquerors in Christ Jesus!

 What, then, shall we say in response to these things? If God is for us, who can be against us? He who did not spare his own Son, but gave him up for us all—how will he not also, along with him, graciously give us all things? . . . "For your sake we face death all day long; we are considered as sheep to be slaughtered." No, in all these things we are more than conquerors through him who loved us. (Romans 8:31-32, 36-37 NIV)

I want to encourage each person who lays eyes on these words: Trust God for all of it! Take hold of the promises written in His Word! This situation—whatever you are facing—is not forever! What seemed to me like a long time while going through it was really just a blink of an eye now. Looking back, it was a moment in time . . . a trial that I had to go through. You might be going through something right now, but the important thing to remember is that you are going through. There is an end to all things and God does know the end from the beginning.

CHAPTER 31

The Scan

From: Sandy O
To: Lorraine
Date: March 15, 2016 6:44 PM
Subject: Praying for your scan

Praying for your scan tomorrow, Lorraine! Praying that you'll be able to "Gaze at God" during the scan to keep your mind centered on Him.

Love you!
Sandy

From: Lorraine
To: Sandy O
Date: March 15, 2016 8:38 PM
Subject: Re: Praying for your scan

Thank you so much Sandy! I will stay focused on the Lord.

You are such a blessing to me!!!

I love you,
Lorraine

From: Julie A
To: Lorraine
Date: March 16, 2016 5:17 AM
Subject: Wednesday

Dear Lorraine,

Letting you know you are thought of on this special day!

Our Bible study circled you in prayer last night and are doing so all week. But today especially there are 9 women of God holding you in their thoughts and prayers.

Sending you love and blessings.

xoxo
Julie

From: Lorraine
To: Julie A
Date: March 16, 2016 8:37 AM
Subject: Re: Wednesday

Thanks so much Julie! You are precious. I appreciate your prayers and your love!

Love you! xoxo

From: Kathy S
To: Lorraine
Date: March 16, 2016 5:25 AM
Subject: Prayers for today

Lorraine~

Asking God our Father to give you a deep sense of his loving presence today. "I will not leave you as orphans; I will come to you" (John 14:18 NIV).

In His love,
Kathy

From: Lorraine
To: Kathy S
Date: March 16, 2016 9:14 AM
Subject: Re: Prayers for today

Thank you so very much Kathy! I feel your prayers! I love you! xoxo

From: Harry
To: Lorraine
Date: March 17, 2016 10:14 AM
Subject: Your scan

Lorraine . . . I know you must have so much going on right now. I know also that this is about the time you would be getting word of the chemo results . . . and I know you will be sharing with us soon. We love you dearly and are continuing to hold you close in our prayers . . . especially now. While we wait to hear from you, I wanted to send you an encouraging word from the Lord . . .

> Through the Lord's mercies we are not consumed, Because His compassions fail not. They are new every morning; Great is Your faithfulness. "The LORD is my portion," says my soul, "Therefore I hope in Him!"
> (Lamentations 3:22-24 NKJV)

From: Lorraine
To: Harry
Date: March 17, 2016 12:45 PM
Subject: Re: Your scan

Thanks so much Harry! Yesterday went well and they said I should hear the results from my doctor in 24-48 hours. I'm feeling good and encouraged by God's Word. As David did, I encourage myself in the Lord. God has pointed me to so many scriptures that relate to my circumstances and I stand firmly for healing and health.

I hope you are having a great day. It's nice and sunny here!

Bless you, dear friend!
Lorraine

From: Sandy O
To: Lorraine
Date: March 17, 2016 12:52 PM
Subject: Hi!

Hi Lorraine!

How did your scan go?

From: Lorraine
To: Sandy O
Date: March 17, 2016 12:58 PM
Subject: Re: Hi!

Hi Sandy,

It went well. I arrived at 1:00, drank two luscious blueberry barium shakes, then at 2:30 they took me back for the scan. They injected the hot iodine dye and the scan was done in less than 5 minutes. They said I should hear the results from my doctor in 24-48 hours. I do recall last time I had a scan, they did it on a Wednesday and then heard from the dr. on Friday.

Standing firmly in faith for my healing!!!

I hope you are having a great day. It's a pretty day!
Love you!

CHAPTER 32

The Result

From: Lorraine
To: All
Date: March 18, 2016 1:09 AM
Subject: CT Result

Dear Family and Friends,

Great news! My CT scan came back NORMAL! NO CANCER! HALLELUJAH!!!!

I'm so overjoyed right now! I've been dancing around the apartment, giving praise to our Lord, our healer, our source of all things!

The doctor called me at 1:33 this afternoon, but I was busy cooking. I had the ringer on my land line turned off (we get so many wrong numbers, we just leave the ringer off now and we rely on the caller i.d. that comes up on our TV). Well, I didn't have the TV on and didn't realize that the doctor called! He left me a voicemail with the good news! It wasn't until 11:00 p.m. when I was getting ready for bed that I noticed the message-waiting light blinking on our phone, and sure enough I had a message. I thought . . . do I check it now or do I just go to bed? Well, I'm so glad I checked it!!!!

Fortunately Greg was still awake and I was able to share this great news with him. We are both so happy! We prayed and praised God together. We are going to have such a sweet celebration!

Thanks for standing with me in this and being with me every step of the way! As I've said many times, God has blessed me with compassion and mercy through each of you. The many ways you have reached out to me during this time have been a source of great encouragement and strength to me. Thank you for allowing to me to see the beauty within each of your hearts. Thank you for being vessels for God's love to me through you! Praise the Lord, Our Healer! And I love the timing . . . that it is leading into Holy Week! What a beautiful time to celebrate new life . . . new birth . . . resurrection! I feel as though I've been born again . . . again! Resurrected into a brand-new start . . . life begins anew! Thank You, Jesus!

Yipppppppeeeeeeeeeeee!!!

Love,
Lorraine / Rainie xoxoxooxoxo

 O Lord my God, I cried to You for help, and You have healed me.
(Psalm 30:2 AMP)

From: Melissa
To: Lorraine
Date: March 18, 2016 1:28 AM
Subject: Re: CT Result

Hoooooorayyyyyyy!!!! Oh Lorraine, I'm so very happy for you!!! And Greg too!!
Thank You, Lord!!! I'm celebrating with you and dancing (quietly :-)) around
the kitchen in joy over your beautiful news right now!!! Praise the Lord who
heals all of our diseases and makes our feet like hinds' feet to walk upon our
high places!!!! Have I got a hug for you, dear sister!!! :-) Love, praise, and blessing be unto the King!!!! – Melissa

---

From: Lorraine
To: Melissa
Date: March 18, 2016 1:31 AM
Subject: Re: Re: CT Result

Oh, I'm so glad you were up to see this! But of course you are! Not only are we
birthday sisters . . . we are late-night sisters . . . kindred spirits!

I love you sweet sis! I can't wait to get that hug! I've got one for you too!

I hope I can sleep now! I'm tired but wired . . . hehe!

Can't wait to celebrate with you! xoxoxo

From: Dr. Kehoe
To: Lorraine
Date: March 18, 2016 3:54 AM
Subject: Re: CT Result

Lorraine,

What fabulous news!! You are a living testimony to the power of prayer. Have a great weekend.

Thanks for keeping me in the loop. This is a truly inspirational story.

Bill

From: Dan
To: Lorraine
Date: March 18, 2016 5:35 AM
Subject: Re: CT Result

Praise God from whom ALL blessings flow!

How awesome!!! Thank You, Lord, for healing Your precious daughter.

We love you and are so very happy for this greatest of news! ☺

Love,
Dan & Jane

From: Gale
To: Lorraine
Date: March 18, 2016 6:08 AM
Subject: Re: CT Result

Lorraine,

What a beautiful morning it is!!

Gale

From: Jane
To: Lorraine
Date: March 18, 2016 6:30 AM
Subject: Re: CT Result

Hallelujah!! Praise God from whom all blessings come!

What blessed news to wake up to! Tears of joy stream down my face as I thank God for you, Greg, and answered prayer! So many lives have been touched by you and your walk thru this journey and I know many more will be touched by this answered prayer. Go celebrate and we can't wait to see you on Sunday!

Love, hugs, and kisses!
Jane

From: Lorraine
To: Jane
Date: March 18, 2016 6:40 AM
Subject: Re: Re: CT Result

Thank you Jane! It was such a great feeling, my emotions didn't know whether to laugh or cry . . . it was a combination of both . . . JOY, JOY, JOY!!! We are looking forward to seeing you and celebrating all of life!!! I love you! xoxo

From: Sandy O
To: Lorraine
Date: March 18, 2016 6:48 AM
Subject: Re: CT Result

THAT IS AWESOME NEWS!!!!! THANK YOU, GOD!!!

It is such good timing . . . to celebrate Jesus's conquering death and His resurrection along with conquering your cancer!!!

You MUST do something FUN to celebrate! What time did you finally go to sleep after celebrating? ☺

From: Lorraine
To: Sandy O
Date: March 18, 2016 7:06 AM
Subject: Re: Re: CT Result

I couldn't sleep for the longest time, and after sending out updates to every-one, it was after 1:00. I was lying in bed for a while before I fell asleep . . . pray-ing and thanking God! The last time I looked at the clock it was almost 2:00. I'm so tired today and too tired to dance, although I'm still dancing on the inside! I need more rest. I trust that my blood counts won't be affected and the joyful reason for this lack of sleep will result in strength.

We will have a huge celebration with family on Palm Sunday and then leave Monday for St. Augustine! When we planned it, Greg said, "We are going no matter what but we are believing all is well." Last night he said, "Now we can go and really relax and celebrate!"

Praise the Lord!

I love you, sweet sister!
Lorraine

From: Liz
To: Lorraine
Date: March 18, 2016 7:09 AM
Subject: Re: CT Result

Lorraine,

I read this wonderful news this morning at 4:25 am when Brad & I got up to go to the gym. We knelt beside the bed and lifted prayers of thanksgiving up for you. We are so overjoyed for this news!!! Brad commented that we gals will have much to celebrate when we get together for our lunch on April 9th.

We continue to trust this healing will be for good and there will never be another time you will have to go through this again!

Love, Liz

From: Missy
To: Lorraine
Date: March 18, 2016 7:11 AM
Subject: Re: CT Result

I can scarcely describe the joy and relief I feel. Tears are filling my eyes in gratitude. I am overjoyed for both of you. Can't wait to you give you a hug!

Love you both so much,
Missy

From: Shelly
To: Lorraine
Date: March 18, 2016 7:51 AM
Subject: Re: CT Result

Lorraine!!!!

Can you hear me screaming??? Praising God?!!

Yesterday if I saw that light blinking, I would've ripped the phone off the wall! Your ease amazes me. :-) I was praying all day—frankly a huge mountain of spiritual warfare against me. I took a vow of silence during the day. Sweet Val, ever so sensitive, joined me in prayer for you and kept saying, "No news is good news." That from the newspaperman.

And now this beautiful report!

Bless God. Bless God. His mercies endure forever!

Oh how your walk has revealed a heart right with God. Bless you! Bless Greg! I pray for fresh and new beginnings. For God's hand to reveal His mysteries and direct your path. He has much in store for you. Shout from the mountains!!!!

 "Consecrate yourselves, for tomorrow the Lord will do amazing things among you."
(Joshua 3:5 NIV)

Your friend for life—
Shelly

From: Lorraine
To: Shelly
Date: March 18, 2016 8:48 AM
Subject: Re: Re: CT Result

I thought that was you . . . boy what great lungs you have! ;)

Thank you so much, sweet sister! Yes, Glory to God!

I was so happy, I had a hard time getting to sleep. Tired today . . . too tired to dance, but I'm dancing on the inside!

I love you both and thank the Lord for your tenderness toward me and your constant encouragement and prayers! Thank you! xoxoxoxo

---

From: Harry
To: Lorraine
Date: March 18, 2016 8:59 AM
Subject: Re: CT Result

My eyes are tearing up with relief and joy. Lorraine, I don't even know what to say except, "Glory to God!" Just like our Lord, you have stepped through the sorrow of the fallen . . . but this morning you are walking into the joy of the risen! I will echo what my last email said: "Weeping may endure for a night, but joy comes in the morning" (Psalm 30:5 NKJV)!

Good Morning, Lorraine! Yes . . . it is a Good Morning!

We rejoice with YOU!

In God's Love and resurrection power,
Harry

From: Julie A
To: Lorraine
Date: March 18, 2016 9:38 AM
Subject: Re: CT Result

There goes God again, showing off!!! Yessssssss!!!!!! Hallelujah!!!!!!! Thank You, God!!!! You are the Alpha and Omega, the beginning and the end!!! The author and finisher of our faith!!! The great I AM. Master, teacher, healer. We bow down and worship You now and forever. God, You are most high and lifted up!!!! Thank You for divine healing. Your mercies are new every morning!!!!!!

Lorraine, I am elated and thankful to our God for His hand in your life. He heard your prayers. He heard all of our prayers. How He loves to surprise and delight us!

On this beautiful day of celebration, get outside in this beautiful sunshine and join me as I shout at the top of my lungs in praise and thankfulness. We have a God who is so much bigger than we could ever imagine.

I can't wait to see you and give you the biggest hug ever. In the meantime, have a wonderful Easter season. Thank you for inspiring me with your faith. You have helped me grow as you've given Him glory and honor all along the way.

Love you dear sister!
xoxo
Julie

From: Pastor Steve
To: Lorraine
Date: March 18, 2016 9:48 AM
Subject: Re: CT Result

Lorraine and Greg, this is such wonderful news and we celebrate with you and praise the Lord for bringing you through such a trial. Lorraine, may I just say what an inspiration and encouragement you have been to me as I watched you go through this time and continually entrust yourself to the Lord. Thank you for that. God bless you both.

In Him,
Steve

Weeping may

endure for a night,

but joy comes

in the morning.

PSALM 30:5 NKJV

From: Aunt Betty and Uncle Orville
To: Lorraine
Date: March 18, 2016 9:53 AM
Subject: Re: CT Result

DEAREST Rainie,

We will all shout Hallelujah together on Sunday! What wonderful news! My eyes puddled up overflowing with joy and relief. Hang on tight 'cause you are going to be smothered in Hugs!

Love Always,
Aunt Betty and Uncle Orville

From: Jim
To: Lorraine
Date: March 18, 2016 11:07 AM
Subject: Re: CT Result

Dear Lorraine,

Indeed, born again . . . again!!

Wonderful news indeed and such a sweet story.

Thank you for sharing your journey and most of all your spirit, your love of God and Jesus, with your friends. We are blessed and inspired by your courage and openness.

Peace be with you.
And all.
Jim

From: Lorraine
To: Jim
Date: March 18, 2016 11:20 AM
Subject: Re: Re: CT Result

Thanks so much Jim! I'm so grateful. I'm thankful to you also, for your constant encouragement, not only through this ordeal, but throughout the years! I look forward to talking to you soon.

We are going to St. Augustine for a few days between Palm Sunday and Easter . . . looking forward to some salt air and sunshine!

Bless you richly!
Lorraine

From: Nori
To: Lorraine
Date: March 18, 2016 11:22 AM
Subject: Re: CT Result

Praise God, Praise God, Praise God.

This is the best news I have gotten in a long while. Thank you for sharing it with me. I will share this great news in my Bible study class tonight. This is definitely a time to celebrate and a time of thanksgiving. Please keep me posted on your next checkup. Let's get together soon and have lunch. Have a great weekend.

Love you!

From: Pastor Bill
To: Lorraine
Date: March 18, 2016 11:34 AM
Subject: Re: CT Result

Lorraine,

Carmé and I were thrilled to hear this news! We praise the Lord with you.

I just want to say again how blessed I was by the way you honored the Lord through this process. Your confidence in Him, your desire to be used by Him to love and pray for others, your sharing of meaningful scripture—all were a blessing to read. Thank you.

For His glory,
Bill

From: Pam (Angel/Jill) ;)
To: Lorraine
Date: March 18, 2016 1:03 PM
Subject: Re: CT Result

:):):):) . . . . amen . . . . exhaling with a huge big smile and restful praise for the Lord! love reading the replies of JOY, too!! Such good news:):):):). May you exhale in peace and rest yourself, Angel—you and Greg both! :) xoxoxoxoxoxo

I'll continue to keep praying for each of us and our needs/requests in the coming months.

love you all,
Pam (Angel/Jill) ;)

From: Laura and Kyle
To: Lorraine
Date: March 18, 2016 1:09 PM
Subject: Re: CT Result

Aunt Lorraine,

Just wanted to express our joy to you!! My parents sent along your email this morning! What awesome news. Kyle and I have been keeping you and Uncle Greg in our thoughts and prayers. So glad all of our prayers have been answered! Looking forward to seeing you this weekend!

Love you,
Laura and Kyle

From: Heather
To: Lorraine
Date: March 18, 2016 2:25 PM
Subject: Re: CT Result

Chills and tears! I am so happy for both of you!!!

Love to you both!
Heather

From: Natalie
To: Lorraine
Date: March 18, 2016 3:14 PM
Subject: Re: CT Result

This Easter celebration is going to be even better with this news to shout out. I have tears of happiness (and relief ;)) flowing but I always knew you'd make it thru this with your faith and strength. Congratulations and HUGE hugs . . . and Happy, Happy Easter from my mom and me!

XOXOXO
Natalie

From: Susie
To: Lorraine
Date: March 18, 2016 7:51 PM
Subject: Re: CT Result

Oh Rainie,

Hallelujah!!! I am crying like a baby! This is awesome! I knew it, I just felt it in my heart! God is Great! I'm so elated with your news and can hardly contain my excitement! I wish I were with you and we would dance all over the place!! How sweet is the mercy and healing of our God! Amen!

I can't imagine what's going through your whole body right now, but I know it's all good!

Happy March 16th! The day you can begin your life again, as you said your life has been renewed!

God Bless you Rainie!

Put your pretty little self at ease, rest your beautiful mind, and praise the Lord!

I love you so so much!!

Celebrate with your sweet husband. I know he's thanking God for healing his girl.

All my love and I will continue praying for you and giving thanks to God. Big hugs and kisses sweet cousin! ☺ Sus

---

From: Beth
To: Lorraine
Date: March 18, 2016 10:55 PM
Subject: Re: CT Result

Oh Rainie!!!!

I am thrilled beyond words!!! I love you and I am so happy for you! I am dancing around too!!! This is the best email EVER!!!!

XOXOXOXOXOXOXO
Beth

From: Debby
To: Lorraine
Date: March 20, 2016 8:41 PM
Subject: Re: CT Result

I am deliriously happy for you, Lorraine!!! What a great God we serve and love. You are so courageous and full of faith. You never faltered once. What a beautiful testimony of the love between you and God. I hope you will do something phenomenal to celebrate. God received so much glory during this trial.

Love you big!
Debby

From: Mariellen
To: Lorraine
Date: March 20, 2016 9:05 PM
Subject: Re: CT Result

Lorraine! Praise God! Praise God! I am dancing with you as well! A blessing, a personal miracle, God's amazing love!

We are so thrilled to hear this news!

Love to you and Greg!

From: Marla and Doug
To: Lorraine
Date: March 20, 2016 9:57 PM
Subject: Re: CT Result

Rainie,

Fantastic news! We are so very happy for you and pray for your continued good health.

God is good. Go dance in His beautiful sunshine!

Doug & Marla ☺

From: Lorraine
To: ALL
Date: March 22, 2016 9:00 AM
Subject: Re: Re: CT Result

Thank you for your constant prayers throughout this journey and even your ongoing prayers in the months ahead. I'll go every three months for follow-up visits and my first visit will be in May.

How do I put into words the love I feel for all of you? How do I repay you for the time and energy and love and goodness you each shared with me out of the grace given to you by God who loves each of you with a depth unseen to the natural man? Your words lifted me up so often! You were an army of God-given soldiers! Your encouragement had much more meaning than you may think. You helped me navigate this journey and stay on course and some of your emails came in at just the right time.

Oh, yes, I made the decision to stay positive and not allow doubt to enter into my thinking or feelings. That said, doubt did try! Fear kept lurking like one of those pesky little bugs. I think they call them "no-see-ums"? Well, it's true . . . you can't see doubt. You can't see fear. You can feel them, though. You can if you let them win. But God's Word says to take all thoughts captive unto Christ Jesus!

> Casting down imaginations, and every high thing that exalteth itself against the knowledge of God, and bringing into captivity every thought to the obedience of Christ.
> (2 Corinthians 10:5 KJV)

Regardless of what we face in life, we all go through things. The key is to remember that we do go through to the other side. Fearful thoughts and doubts will come, but just like those "no-see-ums," we need to swat them away!

We can't see faith either . . . at least in the natural. But we stand firmly in the knowledge of God's Word. There is a supernatural power that is alive in the Word of God and this power is available to each of us if we take it. God offers it freely . . . just as I said in the beginning of this journey, when I experienced God speaking to me about faith. He offers us salvation through His Son, Jesus Christ, and it is ours if we take it. In the same way He offers us healing. It takes faith, and faith comes by hearing and hearing by the Word of God, like it says in Romans 10:17.

Though we can't see faith with our natural eyes, we can see it with our spiritual eyes and we should never swat it away. It is a valuable gift from God. We can give life to fear or we can choose to give life to faith. We can have God's grace (**G**od's **R**iches **A**t **C**hrist's **E**xpense) if we reach out in faith and take it.

Now faith is the substance of things hoped for, the evidence of things not seen.
(Hebrews 11:1 KJV)

I think you know this but I want to proclaim it again and again . . . so I shout it out and proclaim the works of the Lord!

I shall not die, but live, and declare the works of the Lord.
(Psalm 118:17 KJV)

I had fainted, unless I had believed to see the goodness of the Lord in the land of the living.
(Psalm 27:13 KJV)

I have seen the goodness of God in the land of the living! In countless ways! Day in and day out! Every time I received an email or a text, card, gift, phone call, etc., I was experiencing the goodness of God. Your willingness to act on His words; to listen to His promptings; to speak truth, faith, and love into my circumstance, was an act of obedience to His command to love others as you love yourself and to love the brethren as He first loved you!

I have seen the goodness of God in each of you! Please remember this! Please don't let time or the everyday routines of life dampen your spirits . . . ever! Please remember the goodness you helped me to see and take that goodness into the land of the living on a regular basis, encouraging anyone you can! Love them! Look for ways to bless them. You have been blessed to be a blessing!

Greg and I both thank you and stretch our arms up to heaven as if to hug each of you in the spirit. We lift you up to our Father who created you to love. We ask Him to shower you with His blessing and to let you grasp the breadth and length and height and depth of His love!

Thank you for celebrating this great blessing with us! Right now we are packing for a quick trip to St. Augustine for some salt air and sunshine. We planned it before we had the results. Greg said, "We are going to Florida!" Right after we heard the great news, he said, "Now we can really relax and celebrate the right way." Thank the Lord! We are leaping with joy!

"But for you who fear my name, the Sun of Righteousness will rise with healing in his wings. And you will go free, leaping with joy like calves let out to pasture."
(Malachi 4:2 TLB)

God bless you all!

Love,
Lorraine/Rainie

P.S. Praying that you all have a blessed-beyond-measure Easter as you celebrate the resurrection of our Lord. Praising Him for eternal life and life abundant. IN HIM!

CHAPTER 33

Good Friday—A Very Good Friday!

From: Lorraine
To: All
Date: March 30, 2016 12:56 PM
Subject: A Very Good Friday

Hi friends and family!

We returned home Saturday evening from St. Augustine. Before we left on our trip, we were able to spend Palm Sunday with Greg's side of the family and we returned just in time for Easter to spend it with my brother and his family. We had very nice visits with both.

We are back to normal life now. Though it's always wonderful to get away, it's a comforting feeling being back home.

St. Augustine was very nice. We spent a great deal of time just sitting and staring at the water. The B&B was right on the gulf with a gorgeous water view. As always, I was snapping endless photos of the sunset and the water. We were "unplugged" for a few days to rest and to celebrate the miracle in my life. We had a lovely time but wish it would have been longer.

The highlight of our week was Good Friday. We were looking for a nondenominational church to visit and worship and acknowledge the amazing significance of Good Friday. Instead we were blessed to find (out of the blue) a lovely boutique that was Christian owned and we had a wonderfully blessed encounter with the Lord there. Initially we had not seen the shop. We were walking through town and I was suddenly swept inside. Greg said it was as if a magnet just pulled me in. Well, sometimes that's how the Holy Spirit works! He pulled me right into an atmosphere of praise!

The store has an area set up with a "Prayer Wall" where people can write out prayer requests or praises. It is in the center of the store, and people from all around leave prayer requests on a card that they hang from the beautiful wall.

162

It was covered with the unique cards containing their requests or the words of thanks to God for whatever was on their heart.

I was browsing all the beautiful items of clothing, gifts, etc., and Greg had already found the wall and written his prayer of thanks to the Lord for healing me. He showed me his card, which contained the simple but powerful words: "Dear Lord, thank You for healing my wife!" As he watched the expression on my face and my eyes gloss over with tears, he cried. We hugged . . . tight . . . as we thanked God out loud together and the tears streamed down our cheeks. When we turned around, we saw the store owner standing there like an angel witnessing our tears of joy. We shared our story with her. She said, "I want to pray with you." We joined hands and we each prayed . . . for my healing/for us/for her/for her store/for everyone who enters there/giving praise to God for His love for us all! This special time was more therapeutic than the sea breeze, the saltwater, or the sunlight, although each were a heavenly blessing to us! This moment was the highlight of our entire trip as we recognized and received it as an appointed time of worship on Good Friday. We will always cherish that gift of celebration and fellowship.

I hope your Resurrection Day was wonderfully blessed. How are you all? I hope all is well and I hope each of the lovely spring days we are experiencing will be just one more reminder of the newness and freshness and fullness of life! New life! Sweet aroma! Ahhhhhh!

I love you all!
Lorraine/Rainie

CHAPTER 34

What Is Normal?

Really . . . what is normal? Is it just settling into the mundane? After more than eighteen weeks of chemo, I wondered: *Do I just settle in for a while and rest? Do I jump right back into my old routine? Do I choose to forge ahead as if nothing ever happened?*

But then I thought: *How could I? After what I've been through, I can't possibly ever be the same. I'm different now in many ways but I'm better! I feel great! I feel healthy! I feel strong! I know that God has a great plan for me. I don't want to miss it! I want to grab hold of the gifts He has put inside of me and use them . . . and not for applause or adoration but for His glory! How can anyone go through this and not be changed? God has given me a new lease on life. I WILL LIVE AND DECLARE THE WORKS OF THE LORD!!! I want to get up each day with a grateful heart filled with expectation of what God has planned for me.*

Even if you haven't been through such an ordeal, don't you want to choose joy and feel happiness? Don't you want to expect His goodness and experience it? God has a plan for each of us. I want to be still enough to hear it! His Word says:

 "For I know the plans I have for you," declares the LORD, "plans to prosper you and not to harm you, plans to give you hope and a future." (Jeremiah 29:11 NIV)

As we thank Him for another day; for opening our physical and spiritual eyes; for His provision, protection, and promises that are true and never fail, let us see His goodness and mercy and feel His presence as He leads us one step at a time toward the divine destiny He has for us.

Nothing can stand between us and God:

What, then, shall we say in response to these things? If God is for us, who can be against us? (Romans 8:31 NIV)

Maybe if we start the day with thanksgiving for even the little things, we will begin to see more of the great things He places right in front of us. Let us count our blessings not only when things are good, but always. God will never leave you nor forsake you. He is a God of promises. He cannot break His promises because He cannot lie!

If you are going through a difficult time, no matter what it is, don't forget about faith! I can tell you that we can't just wish things away. We have to stand in the faith of God, and the way to do that is to know what His Word says. As I mentioned, He cannot lie! He will not lie! He is a holy God. He is a God of communication. He spoke the worlds into existence. He created Adam and Eve to walk with Him and talk with Him in the garden in the cool of the day! He wants our relationship! He wants us to communicate with Him. Prayer is not just making our requests known to God but it is communication. Communication takes a speaker and a listener. If we listen, we will hear Him. He will guide us and He will give us wisdom to navigate through life. God speaks and things happen! The more time we spend with Him, in His Word, the more we will know what to believe and what to speak out about our circumstances.

I encourage you to find the words God has written that pertain to your circumstances and to become intimate with them in order to speak them over your life. Choose to speak blessings. Swat away the negativity that tries to enter in. Resist it with all your might. Stand firm on God's words that are truth and life.

"The words I have spoken to you—they are full of the Spirit and life." (John 6:63b NIV)

My son, pay attention to what I say; turn your ear to my words. Do not let them out of your sight, keep them within your heart; for they are life to those who find them and health to one's whole body. (Proverbs 4:20-22 NIV)

So we have come to know and to believe the love that God has for us. God is love, and whoever abides in love abides in God, and God abides in him. (1 John 4:16 ESV)

If we really believe that God loves us, we will also believe He keeps His promises. When we know that He keeps His promises, we wait with eager expectation for the answers to be revealed. Even if it takes more time than we thought, we don't give up! God never gives up on us! So don't give up on Him!

Focus on the promises of God and not on the problems that are trying to steal you away!

"The thief comes only to steal and kill and destroy; I have come that they may have life, and have it to the full." (John 10:10 NIV)

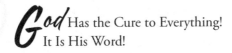

God Has the Cure to Everything!
It Is His Word!

CHAPTER 35

The Word: Always the Same—Me: Forever Changed

Three years prior to this health encounter we had been searching to buy a new home. Our previous home sold in less than a week, and from the time of contract to closing, we had less than thirty days to find a place. We didn't find anything to buy. I informed my husband about a leasing opportunity in a brand-new, beautiful high-rise rental building in the neighborhood of Streeterville in Chicago. I had the idea to rent for a year until we found something to buy, suggesting that in the meantime, we could enjoy living there as if we were in a trendy hotel. He agreed. With the exception of a few pieces of furniture and necessities, we put all of our belongings into storage and moved into our tiny apartment way up high. Little did we know at that time that it would take five summers of looking before we found our next home . . . and little did we know that during that time, I would be faced with a fight for my life! This fight propelled me into the Word of God.

As my body was being immersed in treatment, waiting to be transformed by a powerful medicine, my heart (my spirit) was being transformed by the renewing of my mind. I was hungry . . . thirsty! My main focus was my Bible reading and my time spent alone with God, reading scriptures on faith and healing, listening to sermons, memorizing scriptures that would bolster my faith. I didn't care about time. The beauty of being in that small apartment was that I had the time, as I wasn't distracted by the responsibilities of taking care of a larger home. I wanted to spend as much time with God as possible, absorbing His Word. I needed to know what the Bible said so that I could remain strong and determined, and know without a doubt that He had me! While we were harbored up inside of our apartment (which we affectionately named our "Sky Cottage"—I now refer to it as "The Cocoon"), the Word of God took up residence in my heart like never before.

I focused on this passage, part of which I shared in the previous chapter, but will quote in full here and in another version:

> My son, attend to my words; consent and submit to my sayings. Let them not depart from your sight; keep them in the center of your heart. For they are life to those who find them, healing and health to all their flesh. Keep and guard your heart with all vigilance and above all that you guard, for out of it flow the springs of life. (Proverbs 4:20-23 AMPC)

I wanted what Proverbs said. I wanted to keep God's words in my sight and in the center of my heart. I wanted the life and the healing and health to all my flesh that Proverbs said His words provide! I was vigilant about guarding my heart because I wanted the springs of life to flow out of it and I wanted all of my flesh to be healed. This meant being devoted to God's instruction and believing without any doubt in His promises.

As I made up my mind that I would not allow negativity to enter in, I became more aware of things, words spoken, actions, etc., that were not positive. I would not listen to any news. I wanted only good news so I tuned out anything that might cause stress. God's Word entered in and plucked out any wrong thinking I had, replacing negativity and doubt, lack of faith and weakness with confidence in Him. He plucked out the fear and firmly planted the foundation of faith, which is "the substance of things hoped for, the evidence of things not seen" (Hebrews 11:1 KJV). I may not have been able to see the end from the beginning, but I knew according to His Word that He does know the end from the beginning. I knew that His Word says that I must remain steadfast in His promises and believe Him. As Numbers 23:19 says, He is not a man that He should lie!

As I applied the medicine of His Word to my heart and soul, He made manifest the healing that His Word promises. After months of treatment by way of the application of His written Word and spending time in His presence, as well as the chemo treatment being applied to my body, the cocoon opened, and from it I emerged a new creation. Now I see what I couldn't see then: the reason we had been placed in that apartment for a specific period of time . . . the reason we couldn't find a home for five summers was because that apartment was our place of transformation.

When the time was right, we found a new home. A much larger space—to spread our wings and fly!

It is a new season and we are free in a multitude of ways! I say "we" because my husband and I were both placed in that cocoon together. We learned so much about faith and about remaining planted in God's Word, which is truth, power, healing, provision, protection . . . a safe harbor!

When we look back on that time, we see how God provided for us and how He led us beyond that season. We didn't understand it all then, and we don't understand every detail of it now, but we do know that He never left us to be out there on our own. He came into our presence as we pressed in to Him.

So . . . as I was immersing myself in God's Word and choosing to receive His medicine, I guarded my heart with that life-giving Word, just as I guarded my body with proper nutrition, medicine, exercise, and rest. I chose to "rest" on His promises.

What seemed to be a very long treatment period came to an end more quickly than I had imagined. It was a good end . . . a great end, for which I am eternally grateful! And what seemed to be a very long wait in finding a new home also came to an end . . . another great end.

We emerged from the cocoon into the atmosphere of freedom— transformed from the inside out!

CHAPTER 36

Believing Is Seeing

I want to tell you that faith is not passive. It is an action! We must choose to stand in faith wearing the armor of God as we forge ahead into the battle. We have the freedom to choose. I chose faith and will continue to do so!

I will always remember the voices of those faithful friends and family members who chose to stand in faith with me, encouraging me every step along the way. I will hear my friend Anthony's voice speaking the truth to me and giving me strength in that moment when he told me to take my healing from God, who had already provided it for me at the cross.

I will hear my tender girlfriends' voices as they softly prayed to the Father on my behalf.

I will feel my husband's strong but gentle hand holding mine and walking with me in kindness, goodness, gentleness, and understanding as we were in the battle together. I will reread the words to all of the letters, texts, and cards he gave me throughout. I will remember waking up on the morning of treatment to see his handwriting saying:

Dearest Rainie,

Today God is in full battle mode. He has gone before you to protect and defend His child! You are as strong as an old oak tree whose roots are long and deep. Even the strong winds of life can't shake you. It's God's Word that gives you root. His promises keep you secure. His faithfulness keeps you from being blown to and fro. Think of the beautiful old oak trees in our favorite area of St. Simons. They are 100, 200, or 300 years old and have withstood even hurricane force winds—and yet—they still stand—tall and beautiful. God knows exactly what you need today and He IS with you!

Love, Greg

And another note:

Dearest Rainie,

God has heard every prayer you've prayed. He has seen every tear. He has counted every hair on your head. He has gathered every fiber of your body and touched it with His healing hand! God will carry you through this day. He will answer every prayer with love. He will wipe away every tear and replace it with joy. His healing hand will make you whole, healthy, and strong! You will laugh and dance again!!!

Love, Greg

I want to tell all who are reading this and all who are faced with any hardship: God hears your every prayer too! God is with you! He will also wipe away your every tear and replace it with joy! Yes, YOU WILL laugh and dance again!!! I also want to remind you each of the wise and faithful words of my family doctor, who said exactly what I needed to hear:

You've Got to Believe You're Going to Be OK!

About the Author

LORRAINE BROWN lives in Chicago with her husband, Greg. She has been a writer the majority of her life. As a child, she captured the attention of her fourth-grade teacher, who wanted to publish her first short story. Since that time Lorraine never lost her passion for writing.

She is also an on-camera actress and voice-over talent for television and radio. She is a co-founder of the Chicago Bulls cheerleaders (the Luvabulls) and a former NFL cheerleader for the Chicago Bears (the Honey Bears). Lorraine has many other interests, including a love for photography. She enjoys being creative and capturing the wonder of God's creation in her lens. She is also a published, award-winning poet. She shares many of these interests and her love for life on her website, lorrainebrownauthor.com.

Good News!

The gospel of Jesus Christ is the Good News! All through the Bible, God shows us how much He desires to have a personal relationship with Him. He created Adam and Eve to walk and talk with Him in the garden in the cool of the day. They started out in a perfect, whole relationship with God, but were deceived by satan and gave away their right—their authority—that God had given them, as they fell into sin. Oh, how grateful I am that He provided us with a way back to Him!

> "For God so loved the world that He gave His only begotten Son, that whosoever believeth in Him should not perish, but have everlasting life." (John 3:16 KJ21)

God LOVES you! You can have a personal relationship with your Father in heaven, which He offers you! He craves this relationship with you. He is your GOOD, GOOD FATHER! He made it all possible through Jesus Christ—the one true Savior!

Jesus says: "Here I am! I stand at the door and knock. If anyone hears my voice and opens the door, I will come in and eat with that person, and they with me" (Revelation 3:20 NIV).

The freedom we crave is in Jesus. God sent Jesus to take ALL of our sins upon Himself when He died on that cross. He rose from death on the third day and He ascended to the right hand of the Father. He has been given all power in heaven and on earth! If you truly believe what the Bible says about Jesus and you confess (speak out/declare) that He is Lord, then you can receive the forgiveness and eternal life He has already provided for you . . . and you can enter into a personal relationship with Him.

For it is by grace you have been saved, through faith—and this is not from yourselves, it is the gift of God…. (Ephesians 2:8 NIV)

 If you declare with your mouth, "Jesus is Lord," and believe in your heart that God raised him from the dead, you will be saved. (Romans 10:9 NIV)

 . . . Whosoever shall call on the name of the Lord shall be saved. (Acts 2:21 KJV)

If you have not yet entered into a personal relationship with God through Jesus Christ, and you would like to do so now, simply ask Him into your heart and He will enter. Below is a sample prayer that can guide you as you pray. Do so with a sincere heart and with no doubt that the God who created the heavens and the earth with His mighty power and His outstretched arm, also created you and loves you more than you can comprehend.

> *Heavenly Father, I come to You in the name of Jesus Christ. I believe Jesus is the Son of God, who died for my sins and rose from the dead to give me eternal life. I ask Jesus to come into my heart and to be the Lord of my life from this day forward. I repent of all sin, and I receive Your forgiveness as I commit my life to You. Amen!*

If you have prayed this prayer and received Jesus into your heart, the next step is to get into a Bible-believing church, tell others that you have been born again, and study the scriptures so that you will know and understand the depth of God's love for you as you diligently and earnestly and continually seek after Him!

My prayer for you:

I ask the glorious Father and God of our Lord Jesus Christ to give you his Spirit. The Spirit will make you wise and let you understand what it means to know God.

EPHESIANS 1:17 CEV

AMEN!!!

Made in the USA
Coppell, TX
03 November 2019